GW00938043

006

MANAGING

Health and Safety in

CONSTRUCTION

Construction (Design and Management) Regulations 1994

APPROVED CODE OF PRACTICE AND GUIDANCE

HSE BOOKS

First published 2001

Reprinted 2002, 2004

ISBN 0 7176 2139 1

This guidance is issued by the Health and Safety Executive. Following the guidance is not compulsory and you are free to take other action. But if you do follow the guidance you will normally be doing enough to comply with the law. Health and safety inspectors seek to secure compliance with the law and may refer to this guidance as illustrating good practice.

CONTENTS

Notice of Approval

Approved Code of Practice

This Code has been approved by the Health and Safety Commission, with the consent of the Secretary of State. It gives practical advice on how to comply with the law. If you follow the advice you will be doing enough to comply with the law in respect of those specific matters on which the Code gives advice.

You may use alternative methods to those set out in the Code in order to comply with the law. However, the Code has a special legal status. If you are prosecuted for breach of health and safety law, and it is proved that you did not follow the relevant provisions of the Code, you will need to show that you have complied with the law in some other way or a Court will find you at fault.

Guidance

This guidance is issued by the Health and Safety Commission. Following the guidance is not compulsory and you are free to take other action. But if you do follow the guidance you will normally be doing enough to comply with the law. Health and safety inspectors seek to secure compliance with the law and may refer to this guidance as illustrating good practice.

Notice of Approval

By virtue of Section 16(1) of the Health and Safety at Work etc Act 1974, and with the consent of the Secretary of State for Transport, Local Government and the Regions, the Health and Safety Commission has on 4 September 2001 approved the Code of Practice entitled *Managing health and safety in construction*.

This document contains advice on how to comply with duties under the Construction (Design and Management) Regulations 1994 and, where indicated, on sections 2, 3 and 4 of the Health and Safety at Work etc Act 1974 for work to which those Regulations apply. It contains an Approved Code of Practice (ACoP) which gives advice that has the special legal status described above, and more general guidance, that does not have this special legal status, explaining the law and suggesting ways to comply with it. The ACoP material is shown in **bold type** and additional guidance is shown in normal type. Footnotes and examples do not have ACoP status.

This Code of Practice comes into effect on 1 February 2002. The original Code of Practice under the Construction (Design and Management) Regulations 1994, which came into force on 31 March 1995, is hereby replaced with effect from the same date. A reference in this Code of Practice to another document does not imply approval by the HSC of that document except to the extent necessary to give effect to this Code of Practice.

Introduction

1   The Construction (Design and Management) Regulations 1994 (CDM) came into force on 31 March 1995. They apply to construction work in Great Britain and its territorial sea. This publication contains the Approved Code of Practice (ACoP) and guidance on the duties set out in CDM. It comes into force on 1 February 2002 and replaces the ACoP approved on 3 February 1995 (L54).

2   The construction industry covers a wide range of activities, hazards, materials, techniques, employment patterns and contractual arrangements. In these circumstances, good management of construction projects from concept through to demolition is essential if health and safety standards are to improve. Poor management is a prime cause of the unacceptable accident and occupational health record of the industry.

3   CDM is intended to protect the health and safety of people working in construction, and others who may be affected by their activities. The Regulations require the systematic management of projects from concept to completion: hazards must be identified and eliminated where possible, and the remaining risks reduced and controlled. This approach reduces risks during construction work and throughout the life cycle of a structure (including eventual demolition).

4   CDM brought a major change in construction health and safety, making clients' and designers' duties explicit for the first time. Since then there has been a steep rise in awareness of health and safety, but there have been problems in implementing the Regulations. Those involved with CDM asked for further clear, authoritative guidance setting out practical ways of complying with the Regulations.

5   This revised ACoP and guidance aims to clarify important issues such as the roles of the various dutyholders, how to assess competence and resources, how to prepare health and safety plans, and what should be in the health and safety file.

6   Many people seem to think that CDM requires them to produce paperwork for its own sake. This is far from the truth. CDM is intended to encourage the integration of health and safety into project management. Any paperwork should contribute to the management of health and safety. Work carried out under the Regulations needs to be targeted where it will bring health and safety benefits. If you are asked to do something under CDM which will not produce a health and safety benefit, there is probably a misunderstanding of what the Regulations require. This revision aims to help improve the focus of work carried out, and reduce bureaucracy.

7   In summary, CDM requires:
▼   a realistic project programme with adequate time allowed for planning, preparation and the work itself;

▼   early appointment of key people;

▼   competent dutyholders with sufficient resources to meet their legal duties;

▼   early identification and reduction of risks;

▼   provision of health and safety information from the start of the design phase, through construction and maintenance to eventual demolition, so that everyone can discharge their duties effectively;

▼   co-operation between dutyholders; and

▼   effort and resources proportionate to the risk and complexity of the project to be applied to managing health and safety issues.

8   Most of CDM covers both employees and the self-employed without distinction. People working under the control of others are usually their employees for health and safety purposes, even if they are treated as self-employed for tax and national insurance. Section 3 of the Health and Safety at Work etc Act 1974 (HSWA) and the Construction (Health, Safety and Welfare) Regulations 1996 (CHSWR) also create duties towards the self-employed, and place duties on them. It is important to remember that these legal duties cannot be passed on to someone else by means of a contract.

Managing construction projects
Health and Safety at Work etc Act 1974, Sections 2, 3 and 4

9   Construction work poses serious hazards, for example from asbestos, manual handling, falls, transport and collapses. Each year many people die in accidents and even more suffer ill health. The risks to health and safety from these hazards must be properly controlled. This is particularly challenging because of the number of organisations who need to work together in the rapidly changing environment of a construction project.

10   All those involved must give the management of health and safety a high priority. CDM is part of the equation, but there are other relevant legal requirements. These include duties under HSWA and the Management of Health and Safety at Work Regulations 1999 (the Management Regulations). Building Regulations (in Scotland, Building Standards) also apply to construction work. As well as the duties relating to present and future construction work, there are also duties regarding completed commercial and public buildings which may have implications for design. These include duties under the Workplace (Health, Safety and Welfare) Regulations 1992 and fire precautions legislation.

11   To achieve real improvements in health and safety, hazards must be identified in the early stages of design work. Some can then be eliminated and the remaining risks reduced through good design. Essential information about remaining risks can be passed on in good time to those who are to manage and carry out the work. These people include:

▼   clients, architects, engineers, surveyors, other designers, and other people who decide what is to be constructed, whose decisions can create or eliminate hazards;

▼   contractors, who have to plan their work and co-operate with each other to manage the remaining risks; and

▼ workers, who are at risk of injury or ill health, sometimes many years later.

12 Clients set the tone for the project and have overall control. Their approach is critical to how a project runs in practice. They do not have to manage projects themselves, but must ensure that there are clear and appropriate arrangements for managing and co-ordinating the work of all those involved. Domestic clients are an exception, as they have no legal duties under CDM or HSWA (see section titled *The client*).

13 **Clients, including project originators (paragraph 56), must make appropriate arrangements to ensure that projects are properly managed at all stages. Under the Management Regulations, clients who do not have sufficient knowledge or resources to do this must appoint one or more competent people to help them.**

14 **The client's arrangements must ensure that the structure is designed and constructed so that people carrying out construction work, including upkeep, maintenance and cleaning, can do so safely and without risk to health. The arrangements must also ensure the co-ordination of all measures relating to the health and safety of people affected by the project.**

15 **In particular, the client's arrangements should ensure that:**
(a) **the project allows enough time for design, planning, preparation and construction work, so that the entire project can be carried out safely and without risk to health;**
(b) **the designers and contractors are competent and adequately resourced for the work they have to do;**
(c) **any implications for public safety and for the client's or site occupier's own employees or customers are properly addressed - work near public areas, movement of site vehicles and demolition are examples of the issues that need to be considered;**
(d) **the responsibilities of those who have legal duties, and how they inter-relate, are clear;**
(e) **designers and contractors correctly identify hazards and control measures in accordance with regulation 13 of CDM, regulation 3 of the Management Regulations, and other relevant legislation;**
(f) **there is systematic and routine monitoring and review of the work to ensure that it is undertaken safely and without risk to health; and**
(g) **revisions to designs, programmes of work or method statements are managed safely and without risk to health.**

16 **These arrangements need to be set out in writing in all but the simplest of cases. They should be written simply and clearly, and be as concise as possible. They may be incorporated with other documents, for example the CDM health and safety plan or contracts. Further general guidance on health and safety management is provided in *Successful health and safety management*.**[1]

How to use this publication

17 Appendix 7 provides a summary of CDM duties, with references to appropriate paragraphs elsewhere in this publication.

18 Information on how to comply with the requirements is set out in the following sections of this book. Each section has been written to deal with either the legal duties placed on specific dutyholders or with issues of general interest, but it is important for everyone to understand how the various responsibilities complement one another.

19 The section titled *Application, interpretation and notification* explains the meaning of various terms used in CDM and when CDM applies. For convenience, the full text of the Regulations, as amended, is included at Appendix 1. Key words, phrases and abbreviations are explained in the glossary at Appendix 6.

20 In this book there are a number of lists of issues that dutyholders need to consider. These lists are not exhaustive, and not all the items included are relevant to every project. They are provided to illustrate the sort of issues that those involved often need to consider.

Application, interpretation and notification

Regulations 2 and 3

Does CDM apply to your project?

21 Figure 1 shows where CDM applies.

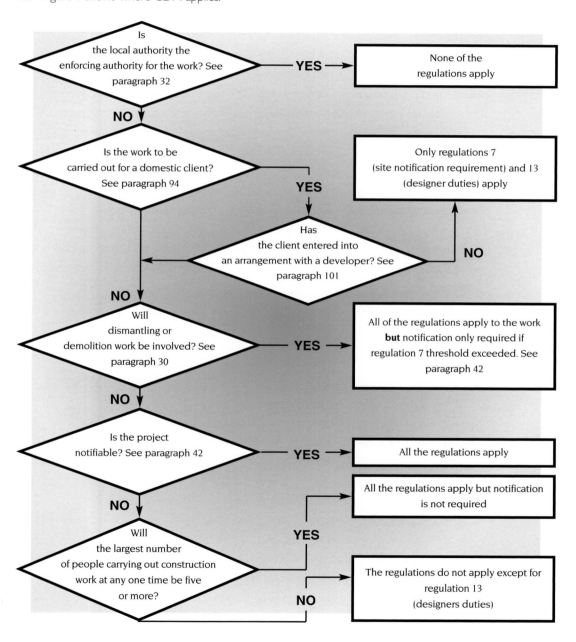

Figure 1 flowchart:

- **Is the local authority the enforcing authority for the work? See paragraph 32** — YES → None of the regulations apply
- NO ↓
- **Is the work to be carried out for a domestic client? See paragraph 94** — YES → **Has the client entered into an arrangement with a developer? See paragraph 101** — NO → Only regulations 7 (site notification requirement) and 13 (designer duties) apply
- NO ↓
- **Will dismantling or demolition work be involved? See paragraph 30** — YES → All of the regulations apply to the work **but** notification only required if regulation 7 threshold exceeded. See paragraph 42
- NO ↓
- **Is the project notifiable? See paragraph 42** — YES → All the regulations apply
- NO ↓
- **Will the largest number of people carrying out construction work at any one time be five or more?** — YES → All the regulations apply but notification is not required; NO → The regulations do not apply except for regulation 13 (designers duties)

Figure 1 Where CDM applies

Interpretation

Cleaning work

22 CDM applies if you are cleaning a structure using water or an abrasive at high pressure, or using corrosive or toxic substances. The cleaning of windows, transparent or translucent walls, ceilings or roofs is also subject to some of the requirements of CDM. Where this work involves a risk of falling more than 2 metres, the requirements on designers (see regulations 13(2)(a) and 13 (2)(b)), and on planning supervisors in respect of the health and safety file (see regulation 14(d)(ii)), apply.

Construction phase

23 The construction phase is the part of the project when construction work takes place. This includes on-site preparations and any demolition. The construction phase ends when construction work on the project finishes. Fitting out or commissioning, whether carried out by a contractor or the client, is included in the construction phase. Where clients directly manage this work, they assume the role of principal contractor.

24 When there is a phased handover of a number of structures, as part of the same project, the construction phase continues until work on the last structure is complete.

25 Snagging usually forms part of the construction phase. Remedial work and repairs after the construction phase has finished are separate projects, and may be separately notifiable, where appropriate.

Construction work

26 Under regulation 2 of CDM, construction work means carrying out building, civil engineering or engineering construction work. This includes:
- associated preparations, cleaning, maintenance (including repair, renovation, upkeep and re-decoration), demolition and dismantling;
- installation, commissioning, decommissioning or dismantling any fixed plant (eg silos, chemical or nuclear reactors, boilers, air-conditioning units, lifts and telecommunications) which involve a risk of someone falling more than 2 metres. 'Plant' is defined in section 53 of HSWA as including any machinery, equipment or appliance. Fixed plant means any plant that is fixed in one position and is not intended to be moved frequently;
- offshore construction within the territorial sea, except for the construction of fixed offshore oil and gas installations at the place where they will be used;
- exploratory work in preparation for construction, including the drilling of exploratory bore holes and investigatory work, but not site surveys;
- construction of temporary structures used during construction work (eg formwork, falsework, scaffolds or other structures providing support or means of access).

27 The following are not construction work:
- putting up and taking down marquees and similar tents designed to be re-erected at various locations;
- maintenance of fixed plant, other than services;
- tree planting and general horticultural work;

▼ archaeological investigations;

▼ positioning and removal of lightweight partitions, such as those used to divide open-plan offices or to create exhibition stands and displays;

▼ erecting scaffolds for support or access in non-construction work;

▼ surveying - this includes taking levels, making measurements and examining a structure for faults;

▼ work to or on vessels such as ships and mobile offshore installations;

▼ manufacture at a factory of items for later use in construction work (eg roof trusses, pre-cast concrete panels, bathroom pods and similar prefabricated elements and components); and

▼ fabricating elements which will form parts of offshore installations.

> **Example 1**
>
> Maintenance work, carried out at a power station during a shutdown, involved de-commissioning, dismantling, re-assembly and re-commissioning of major plant items, together with work on the services and controls, by large numbers of contract workers, often working 24-hour shift patterns over a number of weeks. Although some of the work was not subject to CDM, the client decided to apply the CDM management approach to all of the work to ensure that it was well planned and co-ordinated.

28 Some construction projects include operations which are not themselves construction work (see paragraph 27). Where this is the case, the overlap between the construction and non-construction work should be addressed in the health and safety plan.

29 HSWA and other health and safety legislation (see Further information section at the back of this book) apply whether or not an activity is construction work.

Demolition and dismantling

30 CDM applies to all demolition or dismantling work, whether or not the work has to be notified to the Health and Safety Executive (HSE) (see paragraph 42). Demolition and dismantling includes the deliberate pulling down, destruction or taking apart of a structure, or a substantial part of a structure. It includes dismantling for re-erection or re-use. Demolition does not include operations such as making openings for doors, windows or services or removing non-structural elements such as cladding, roof tiles or scaffolding. These operations may, however, form part of demolition or dismantling work when carried out alongside other activities.

Design

31 CDM applies to all design work for construction, including designs for domestic clients.

Enforcing authority

32 The enforcing authority for health and safety law is HSE in some cases and the local authority in others, as set out in the Health and Safety (Enforcing Authority) Regulations 1998 (HSEAR). The type of activity carried out at the workplace is normally the deciding factor. The user of the workplace should know which enforcing authority covers the premises. HSE or the local authority (usually the Environmental Health Department) can provide further advice. For most construction work, the enforcing authority is HSE.

33 Under Schedule 2 of HSEAR, where the local authority is the enforcing authority for the work normally carried out, HSE becomes the enforcing authority for construction work if:
▼ the work is notifiable under CDM (paragraph 42);
▼ all or part of the work being undertaken by a contractor is to the exterior of the building or structure; or
▼ the work is carried out in a physically segregated area of the premises, where the activities normally carried out have been stopped to enable construction to take place, and the contractor has the authority to exclude people not carrying out construction. This does not include the maintenance (including removal) of insulation on pipes, boilers or other parts of heating or water systems.

34 The local authority remains the enforcing authority where the people doing the work are those who normally work on the premises. HSE is usually the enforcing authority where the local authority is the client.

Non-work activities
35 CDM only applies to construction projects involving people at work. Some construction projects are undertaken by groups of people who are not at work. Examples are self-build groups building homes where they will live, charity volunteers, and community service offenders. However, CDM can apply to these projects if other people also work on them. For example:
▼ a charity may employ people to manage and direct the work done by volunteers;
▼ groups of 'self-builders' may form a company to administer the work on behalf of the group. They may then hire professionals to do some operations, eg specialist ground work contractors. The specialist would be at work and the work would be for the company and not a domestic client.

Projects
36 A project includes all the preparation, design, planning and construction work required to achieve the end result desired by the client. Many projects involve several structures.

37 In some cases where there are substantial breaks in the work between phases it may be appropriate to treat each phase as a separate project. For example, a structure may be demolished long before construction starts on the cleared site. In these circumstances the demolition is normally considered a project in its own right. Similarly, works such as the diversion of services well in advance of the next phase may be treated as a separate project.

38 Some projects go through distinct phases, each of which requires a different set of skills to manage health and safety effectively. One approach is to appoint a principal contractor from the outset who has the range of skills required to manage and co-ordinate all phases of the work. Alternatively, a different principal contractor can be appointed for each phase. Clients should ensure that the position of principal contractor is filled at all times, and that there is only one principal contractor for a project at any one time. The key is to ensure that the right people are in place at the right time and that there is a clear hand-over of responsibility. The section titled The principal contractor provides further guidance on this role.

Term contracts

39 CDM does not necessarily apply to arrangements such as fixed-term contracts over a long period, typically for maintenance or emergency work. The application of CDM to each block of work under these kinds of contract needs to be considered individually.

Utilities

40 Utility companies carry out a variety of CDM roles and they may fulfil more than one role on some projects. They normally arrange for work to be done and are in the best position to ensure that designers and contractors doing the work are competent, as required by regulation 8(3). Utilities frequently operate on sites as designers and/or contractors. When they do so, they must provide the principal contractor with relevant information about hazards arising from their designs or operations, and about how the resulting risks are to be controlled. Similarly, they must be given relevant information on the risks to their health or safety arising from the construction work. This exchange of information is straightforward in most cases. Utility companies must accept the authority of the principal contractor and the importance of the principal contractor's co-ordinating role, and must comply with relevant site rules.

Work outside Great Britain
Regulation 20

REGULATION 20

41 CDM applies to work carried out within Great Britain and certain activities in its territorial sea, for example, construction of an offshore wind farm. People working abroad have no duties under CDM, but the law still applies to clients in Britain who choose to use designers or others working abroad. These clients must make sure that those they engage are competent; that health and safety issues are properly considered; and that the normal CDM information is provided. This can be covered in contracts.

Notification
Regulations 2(4) and 7

REGULATIONS 2(4) & 7

42 Details of some projects which CDM applies to must be notified to HSE. This is the case where construction work is expected to:
▼ last more than 30 days; or
▼ involve more than 500 person days.

43 Any day on which work takes place counts towards the period of construction work, including weekends and holidays. The total 'person days' is the total number of shifts worked by everybody involved in the project, including supervisors. In borderline cases, where you are unsure how long the work will take, it is best to notify HSE.

44 Where a small project, which was not notifiable, requires a short extension or small increase in the number of people, you do not need to notify HSE of the change. However, construction work may significantly overrun or the scope may change so that it becomes notifiable. If this happens you must notify HSE as soon as you can.

45 Figure 2 sets out when to notify HSE.

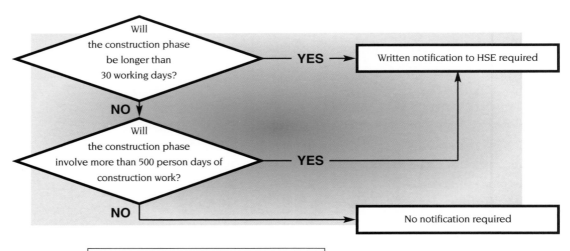

| **Figure 2** When to notify HSE |

REGULATION 7

Regulation 7

46 The planning supervisor is responsible for making sure HSE is notified, except where work is carried out directly for domestic clients (see paragraph 94). A contractor working directly for a domestic client is responsible for notifying HSE of the work. Where several contractors are working together on a domestic project, one of them can notify HSE on behalf of the others.

47 The information needed in a notification is set out in Schedule 1 of CDM. Form 10(rev), available from HSE's local offices and reproduced at Appendix 5, may be used to notify HSE. You do not have to use it, as long as you provide all of the specified information.

48 Regulation 16(1)(d) requires a copy of the notification to be clearly displayed on the site (see paragraph 175).

49 Notification must be sent as soon as possible after appointing the planning supervisor, which should be at the start of design work (see paragraph 75). (When working for domestic clients, the contractor must notify HSE before work begins.) Notification should not be delayed because some of the information is unavailable, for example, if a principal contractor has not yet been appointed. The missing information must be notified once it becomes available; when doing so, it is helpful to make clear that is additional notification. In all cases full details must be sent to HSE before construction starts. It is helpful to notify HSE if there are any significant changes, for example when a new principal contractor is appointed.

50 Where work is for a domestic client, there is no requirement for a planning supervisor. Contractors must, however, notify HSE before work begins. If a developer undertakes construction work for a domestic client then a planning supervisor is required (see paragraph 101). Only those details that are relevant need to be included in the notification.

51 Notification should be sent to the HSE office that covers the site where the construction work is to take place. Addresses of HSE's local offices and the areas they cover can be obtained from HSE's Infoline (08701 545500) or HSE's website www.hse.gov.uk.

The client

52 CDM is designed to promote a systematic approach to the management of health and safety in construction. Clients have a key role to play in this, as they set the tone of a project and make decisions crucial to its development. The intention is to ensure work carried out for them is conducted with proper regard to the health and safety of workers and others. That is why CDM places explicit duties on clients requiring them to select competent people, provide relevant information, and ensure there are adequate resources, including time, for each stage of the work. These all contribute to a well-planned approach to health and safety.

53 Because clients may know little about construction health and safety, the Regulations require designers to make them aware of their duties. Planning supervisors should also be able to advise clients. Clients can appoint a competent agent to carry out their remaining duties under CDM. This agent could be one of the other CDM dutyholders.

54 Effective implementation of CDM should benefit clients through:
▼   improved planning and control of projects, reduced delays from unforeseen problems or abortive work, and more reliable costings and completion dates;
▼   reduced overall cost of ownership because the structure is designed for safe and easy maintenance and cleaning work, and because key information is available in the health and safety file - a recent study found that the typical maintenance costs of a building are five times the construction costs;[2]
▼   improved communication between key parties; and
▼   a reduction in accidents and ill-health among construction workers and in associated costs, delays and bad publicity.

55 Clients have the greatest influence on the time available for the project and should allow sufficient time for those they appoint to carry out their duties. The budget for a project must allow adequate resources for it to be carried out safely. These resources include adequate time to prepare the design, and to develop the pre-tender and construction phase health and safety plans. The principal contractor also needs sufficient time to bring together the labour force and equipment, arrange welfare facilities, plan and prepare for the project and carry out the work safely. It is better to have a realistic completion date that can be relied on, than an unrealistic deadline.

Who are clients?
Regulation 2

56 A client is an organisation or individual for whom a construction project is carried out, whether by others or in-house. This means a wide range of bodies may be clients under CDM, eg local authorities, school governors, insurance companies and project originators on Private Finance Initiative (PFI) projects. 'Clients' include agents of clients, and developers (see paragraphs 101-102). Domestic clients are a special case and do not have duties under

CDM (see paragraphs 94-96).

57 In some circumstances it may not be immediately obvious who is legally the client. To avoid confusion, this needs to be resolved at the earliest stage possible by those involved. Factors to be taken into account include:

▼ who is at the head of the procurement chain;

▼ who arranges for the design work; and

▼ who engages the contractors.

Regulation 4(1) to (4)

58 Clients can appoint a competent, adequately resourced agent to carry out their CDM duties, but they retain their other duties under health and safety law, such as ensuring the health and safety of people affected by their work. For the client's remaining duties to be fully transferred to such an agent, the agent must ensure a written declaration is sent to HSE (see regulation 4(4).

59 When a project is carried out for a number of clients, one of the clients, or an agent, may agree to accept the clients' responsibilities on behalf of them all. This can only be done by sending a written declaration with the information required by regulation 4(4) to HSE. However, if agents do not make a declaration, they may still be legally accountable.

What clients must do

Regulations 6, 8, 9, 10, 11 & 12

60 Clients must make timely appointments of competent and adequately resourced:

▼ planning supervisors (see paragraph 73); and

▼ principal contractors (see paragraph 80).

61 There must be one planning supervisor and one principal contractor at all times until the end of the construction phase, including the commissioning stage. Appointments can be terminated, changed or renewed as necessary. The planning supervisor and principal contractor can be individuals or organisations.

62 Clients must also:

▼ satisfy themselves that the designers, or other contractors they employ, are competent and

> ## Example 2
>
> A developer funded improvements and alterations to the highway as a part of a major shopping development. The improvements and alterations had to satisfy the requirements of the highway authority. In this case the developer engaged all the contractors, and was the only client.

> ## Example 3
>
> A client wished to appoint a design and build contractor for a project. To prepare for this he appointed a competent planning supervisor and designer. The planning supervisor developed the health and safety plan, which was issued to all the contractors who were invited to tender. The tender documents also stated that the successful contractor was to take over the role of planning supervisor and to submit, with their tender, evidence of their competence to do this.

REGULATION 4(1) TO (4)

REGULATIONS 6, 8, 9, 10, 11 & 12

adequately resourced to carry out their duties under CDM. They also need to consider how these contractors and designers will work with the principal contractor and any lead designer;

▼ provide relevant health and safety information about existing structures and the site (see paragraphs 83-86);

▼ allow sufficient time for the design and construction work to be carried out properly;

▼ ensure that construction work starts only when there is a suitably developed construction phase health and safety plan (see paragraph 87); and

▼ ensure that the project health and safety file is available for any future construction work, and for handing on to a new owner (see paragraph 91).

63 If clients specify materials or methods of working, this may make them designers under CDM, with the additional duties of a designer in relation to those specific matters. Clients must ensure that they understand and fulfil these duties where their requirements have significant health and safety implications.

64 CDM does not require clients to monitor the performance of their appointees. However, clients have duties under section 2 of HSWA if the work of contractors could put their own employees at risk. Clients also have duties regarding the safety of other workers and members of the public under sections 3 and 4 of HSWA. To discharge these duties they may need to make arrangements for monitoring (see paragraphs 9-16). The results of any monitoring also provide good evidence of competency for any similar future projects.

> ## Example 4
>
> A designer specified tilt and turn windows to reduce risks during window cleaning. The client overruled this on the grounds of cost. The designer pointed out that the client was taking over his duties under regulation 13 of CDM, and needed to address how the risk to window-cleaners could be minimised and how the duties under the Workplace Regulations could be complied with.

CDM and contracts

65 Whatever the form of contract or agreement between the parties, it is important for clients to ensure that the appointments required by CDM are made, that its principles are followed, and that arrangements are in place to manage health and safety. Many CDM duties require something to be done, but do not specify who must do it. It is helpful to draft contracts or appointment documents to make sure that these tasks are appropriately and clearly allocated and that everybody is clear about what they have to do.

66 The client and those involved need to agree:

▼ who is to notify HSE about the project;

▼ who is to prepare the pre-tender health and safety plan;

▼ who is to prepare the health and safety file, and in what format; and

▼ whether the planning supervisor will be required to advise the client on:

    ▼ the competence and resources of appointees; and

    ▼ the adequacy of the principal contractor's health and safety plan.

67 If a client appoints a principal contractor without tendering, a health and safety plan is still needed when initial arrangements for construction work are made, so that the contractor knows about the key health and safety issues.

Private finance initiative (PFI) and public private partnership (PPP)

68 Precisely how CDM applies to the early stages of PFI, PPP and similar forms of procurement can be difficult to determine, as these arrangements were not considered when the regulations were drafted. This section is intended to ensure that the aims underpinning CDM are achieved, and is in accordance with the Government's commitment to best practice as a client.

69 The project originator is the client until someone else takes on this role, so they should ensure that there are appropriate arrangements for managing the project (see paragraphs 9-16). This includes ensuring that the roles of all those involved in the project are made clear at all stages, and that adequate time and resources are available to ensure health and safety throughout the project.

70 To meet the aims of CDM it is crucial that early designs and specifications take full account of the principles set out in the section titled *The designer*. If this is left until a contract is awarded it may be too late. Addressing these issues at such a late stage is likely to be ineffective and expensive.

71 Project originators are responsible for any requirements they impose. This may make them designers under CDM, with the additional duties of a designer. They must provide any relevant information to inform the design, and ensure that a pre-tender health and safety plan is provided to bidders.

72 A Special Purpose Vehicle or design-build contractor, once appointed, normally takes over as the client for the remainder of a project.

Appointing the planning supervisor
Regulation 6(1) and (3)

REGULATION 6(1) & (3)

73 A client must appoint a competent, adequately resourced organisation or individual as planning supervisor. This role is explained in the section titled *The planning supervisor*. The planning supervisor may act solely in this role, or may take on the function along with another role, for example, designer or principal contractor. The planning supervisor's main responsibility is to ensure that all those carrying out design work on a project collaborate and pay proper attention to the need to reduce risk wherever possible.

74 Large, complicated projects normally require a greater range of experience and more resources, and there may need to be a team approach for the planning supervisor role. Other projects may be dealt with by an experienced individual who has worked on similar projects and can draw on specialists when necessary. In all cases the planning supervisor needs to have:

▼ a thorough understanding of the design process;

▼ appropriate understanding of construction health and safety; and

▼ appropriate understanding of the type of work involved and of health and safety issues which could arise in future maintenance, refurbishment and demolition.

75 The greatest potential impact of CDM is at the concept and scheme design stages. As a scheme moves into the detailed design stage, it becomes more difficult to make fundamental changes that eliminate hazards and reduce resulting risks. Planning supervisors must be appointed at or before the start of design work if they are to be able to:

(a) advise clients on the competence and resources of their appointees;

(b) ensure that early design decisions fully address the significant health and safety issues;

(c) enable the development of an adequate pre-tender health and safety plan;

(d) enable the health and safety file to be produced in a user friendly format, suitable for future use.

> ### Example 5
>
> On a large contract for a bank, worth several million pounds, the planning supervisor was appointed late and given less than 48 hours to prepare a pre-tender health and safety plan.
> This meant that there was insufficient time to properly consider the plan. Work was delayed because the contractor had no information about the underground services to be found on site. As well as this, the planning supervisor was not able to influence the design.

76 Planning supervisors have a continuing role in relation to design work during the construction phase. Design of permanent and temporary work is often carried out during construction, for example when clients require changes or when unforeseen problems are encountered on site. This is particularly common in refurbishment work. The work of contractors or suppliers also frequently involves additional design work.

Arranging design work
Regulations 8 and 9

REGULATIONS 8 & 9

77 Clients must employ only competent, adequately resourced designers. Designers can be an organisation, an individual, or an in-house design team. Designers must be able to:

▼ identify hazards inherent in their designs;

▼ identify the resultant risks during construction, maintenance or demolition; and

▼ understand how to eliminate the hazards, or reduce the risks.

78 The section titled *The designer* gives more information on the duties of the designer.

79 Clients often employ more than one designer, for example different architects, civil, structural and services engineers. In these cases the appointments need to be timed so that the design work can be co-ordinated from an early stage. In these situations, nominating one

designer as the 'lead designer' often helps to ensure good co-ordination and co-operation. The planning supervisor also has an important role to play in ensuring co-ordination.

Appointing the principal contractor
Regulation 6(1)(b), (2) and (4)

80 Clients must appoint a competent, adequately resourced principal contractor. The principal contractor must be an organisation or an individual who actually undertakes, carries out or manages construction work. The main or managing contractor in overall day-to-day control of the project is often appointed as principal contractor, but clients may also appoint an in-house team, separate company, project engineer or manager. A principal contractor's key duty under CDM is to plan for, and manage, the project to ensure the health and safety of everybody affected by the work, paying special attention to co-ordination and communication. The section titled *The principal contractor* discusses their duties.

81 The principal contractor should be appointed as soon as the client knows enough about the project to select a suitable contractor. Early appointment allows the principal contractor to contribute to the design process, and gives enough time to develop an adequate construction phase health and safety plan and to arrange for appropriate resources, including welfare facilities.

Notifying HSE about appointments
82 If projects are notifiable, HSE must be informed in writing about the appointments of the planning supervisor and principal contractor. The planning supervisor normally notifies HSE (see paragraphs 42-51).

> **Example 6**
>
> A client recognised that welfare facilities were required from the very beginning of the construction phase. This meant services had to be installed early. She arranged with the utilities for these services to be installed at the very start of the construction phase in conjunction with the principal contractor. This reduced the lead time required before construction could begin.

Providing information for projects
Regulation 11

83 Clients must provide the planning supervisor with the information needed to identify hazards, including those arising from previous work, site conditions, and activities on or near the site. They must take reasonable steps to obtain necessary information. This may include carrying out surveys and other investigations.

84 Clients who have previously carried out surveys, or have a health and safety file from earlier work carried out under CDM, should

> **Example 7**
>
> A client proposed to build a new ferry terminal. The client informed the planning supervisor about the operation of the nearby liquefied petroleum gas terminal. The design and health and safety plan took account of the potential impact of shipping operations on the construction project, and enabled risks to the LPG operations to be identified and minimised.

already have relevant information in a suitable form. The planning supervisor can provide advice on the additional information required and should pass this information to the designer.

85 Clients must not leave it to contractors to discover hazards. Relevant information needs to be considered at the design/planning stage by the designer and those preparing the health and safety plan. Without it, the work cannot be properly planned, or decisions made about the resources needed. The information needs to be sufficient to ensure that significant risks during construction can be anticipated, and avoided or properly controlled. It needs to include, for example:

(a) the presence, location and condition of hazardous materials, such as asbestos or waste chemicals;

(b) activities on or near the site, which will continue during construction work, eg retail shops, deliveries and traffic movements, railway lines or busy roads, public access to a retail store;

(c) requirements relating to the health and safety of the client's employees or customers, eg, permit-to-work systems in a petrochemical plant, fire precautions in a paper mill, one-way systems on site, means of escape, 'no-go' areas, smoking and parking restrictions;

(d) access and space problems, such as narrow streets, lack of parking, turning or storage space;

(e) information about means of access to parts of the structure, eg fragile materials and anchorage points for fall arrest systems;

(f) available information about site services and their location, in particular, about those that are concealed, such as underground services;

(g) ground conditions and underground structures or water courses, such as culverts, where this might affect the safe use of plant, eg cranes, or the safety of groundworks, eg the construction of trenches;

(h) buildings, other structures or trees which might be unstable or at risk of unintentional collapse;

Example 8

A client commissioned an asbestos survey before beginning the refurbishment of a 1960s office block. This revealed the presence of amosite asbestos. The results of the survey were passed to the planning supervisor and included in the pre-tender health and safety plan.

Example 9

A client arranged for a section of steel roof sheeting to be replaced because it was leaking. The client did not inform the contractor that an adjacent section of roof contained fragile rooflights. A roofer strayed onto the adjacent roof and fell to his death through a PVC rooflight.

Example 10

A client was aware that there could be high levels of arsenic in the soil in their locality. He arranged for tests to be carried out and found significant levels. The risk at such levels and the need to develop appropriate risk control measures was made clear in the pre-tender plan.

(i) previous structural modifications, including weakening or strengthening of the structure;

(j) fire damage, ground shrinkage, movement or poor maintenance which may have adversely affected the structure;

(k) any difficulties relating to plant and equipment in the premises, such as overhead service gantries whose height restricts access;

(l) health and safety information contained in earlier design, construction or 'as-built' drawings, such as details of pre-stressed or post-tensioned structures.

86   The client must make this information available to the planning supervisor early enough for its implications to be assessed by the designer. Using this information the designer may be able to significantly reduce the risks. Relevant parts of the information must then be included in the pre-tender health and safety plan.

Ensuring there is a health and safety plan for the construction phase
Regulations 9(3) and 10

REGULATION 9(3) & 10

87   A good construction phase health and safety plan is an essential part of effective risk management. It makes delays or increased cost due to unforeseen problems far less likely, and helps identify measures to reduce the risk of injury. The plan often requires considerable work to prepare. Clients must allow adequate time for this.

88   Before construction work begins, clients must ensure that the principal contractor has prepared a project-specific plan that meets the requirements of regulation 15(4) and, in particular, sets out:

▼   the framework for dealing with the management and monitoring of health and safety, emergency procedures, arrangements for communications and provision of welfare facilities; and

▼   the key health and safety issues for the early stages of the project (see paragraphs 233-239).

89   CDM only requires clients to ensure that the plan contains this information. They do not have to approve the plan. Clients may wish to seek advice from the planning supervisor as to whether the plan complies with regulation 15(4), if they do not know enough to judge for themselves.

90   Once the construction phase has begun, neither the client nor the planning supervisor has a duty, under CDM, to check that the plan continues to comply with regulation 15. This is the duty of the principal contractor. However, duties under HSWA continue to apply to the client and planning supervisor (see paragraph 9).

The health and safety file
Regulation 12

REGULATION 12

91   The health and safety file must be finalised and passed to the client as soon as possible, preferably at or before completion of the construction phase. In some cases, for example where there is partial occupation or phased handover of a project, the client may need information

from the file before the whole project is completed. Clients need to make sure that there are appropriate arrangements for collecting and compiling the information that is likely to be needed for the file, and for agreeing a suitable, user-friendly format with the planning supervisor.

92 The purpose of the health and safety file is to provide information for future construction work including cleaning, maintenance, alterations, refurbishment and demolition. So clients need to ensure that the file is available for inspection when this type of work takes place. It is a key part of the information and the client, or the client's successor, must pass it on to anyone preparing or carrying out work which CDM applies to.

93 The health and safety file can provide significant benefits to the client by minimising the cost of future work. So it is well worth the effort to ensure it is kept up to date, even when work not subject to CDM is carried out. The section titled *The health and safety file* gives further information.

Domestic clients

94 Domestic clients are people who have work done which does not relate to their trade or business. This is usually the case where someone commissions work on their own home, or the home of a family member. No duty is placed on domestic clients by CDM or HSWA. It is the type of client that is the key to this exclusion, not the type of property. Local authorities, housing associations, charities, landlords and other businesses or limited companies may own domestic property, but they are not domestic clients. If the work involves a workplace attached to domestic premises, such as a shop, the client is not a domestic client.

95 Sometimes groups who would otherwise be domestic clients form companies to administer construction work. A common example of this is a company formed by leaseholders of flats to undertake maintenance of the common structure. In this case, the company is a client with a client's duties (see paragraph 35).

Duties when work is done for a domestic client

Designers working for domestic clients still have duties under Regulation 13 of CDM to give adequate attention to health and safety when preparing their designs and to provide health and safety information.

96 Contractors are required to notify HSE about projects for domestic clients which last more than 30 days or 500 person days (see paragraph 42). There is, however, no requirement for either a planning supervisor or principal contractor. Neither is there any requirement relating to health and safety plans or files, even when demolition is involved. Other health and safety law still applies. Some of the most relevant legislation is listed in the *Further information* section at the end of this book.

Insurance and warranty claims

97 An insurance company arranging for construction work to be carried out under the terms of an insurance policy is the client for the purposes of CDM. Where the work is arranged by the insured, and the insurance company reimburses them, then the insured is the client. A domestic client has no CDM duties.

98 If the insurer specifies designers or contractors for certain aspects of the work, then the insurer is the client and is responsible for arranging for that company to do the work. The insurer is therefore responsible for establishing that designers or contractors are competent and adequately resourced. The section titled *Competence and resources* provides more information on how to do this.

99 With insurance-related work, it is common for agents to be appointed to act on behalf of either the insured or insurer. These agents resolve claims and may co-ordinate the remedial works and have clients' duties (see paragraph 58). As domestic clients have no duties under CDM, neither does an agent working directly for a domestic client. Agents working for the insurer have duties as clients (see paragraphs 56 and 58).

100 Where remedial work is carried out under a home warranty scheme, such as those provided by the National House Building Council (NHBC), it is the provider of the warranty, eg NHBC, which is the client for the purposes of CDM. Therefore CDM applies to the client in the normal way.

Developers
Regulation 5

101 In some instances, domestic clients may buy a house or flat before the whole project is complete (for example where house builders develop a site with a view to selling a number of homes). In these cases the purchaser may have an interest in the property, but it is still the developer who arranges for the construction work. So the developer remains the client under CDM.

102 Builder-developers are usually both clients and principal contractors, although they may appoint another contractor as principal contractor. They may also be designers and planning supervisors; and may be carrying out their various roles in-house. They must comply with CDM in all their roles.

REGULATION 5

The designer

103 Designers are in a unique position to reduce the risks that arise during construction work, and have a key role to play in CDM. Designs develop from initial concepts through to a detailed specification, often involving different teams and people at various stages. At each stage, designers from all disciplines can make a significant contribution by identifying and eliminating hazards, and by reducing the remaining risks.

104 Designers' earliest decisions can fundamentally affect construction health and safety. These decisions influence later design choices. Considerable work may be required if it is necessary to unravel earlier inappropriate decisions, so it is vital to address health and safety at the very start.

105 Designers' responsibilities extend beyond the construction phase of a project. They also need to consider the health and safety of those who will maintain, repair, clean and eventually demolish a structure. Failure to address these issues adequately at the design stage may make it difficult to devise a safe system of work. It could also cause additional costs later because, for example, expensive scaffolding or other access equipment is needed.

106 Designers have to weigh many factors as they prepare their designs. This section focuses on those that have health and safety implications. These have to be weighed alongside other considerations, including cost, fitness for purpose, aesthetics, buildability and environmental impact.

107 Designers must reduce foreseeable risks to health and safety, based on the information available when the design is prepared or modified. The greater the risk, the greater the weight that must be given to eliminating or reducing it. Designers must not produce designs that cannot be constructed safely.

108 Where risks remain, designers must provide the information needed to ensure that planning supervisors, other designers and contractors are aware of them and can take account of them.

Who are designers?
Regulation 2

REGULATION 2

109 In CDM the term 'designer' has a broad meaning. Designers are those who have a trade or a business which involves them in:
▼ preparing designs for construction work including variations - this includes preparing drawings, design details, specifications, bills of quantities and the specification of articles and substances, as well as all the related analysis, calculations, and preparatory work; or
▼ arranging for their employees or other people under their control to prepare designs relating to a structure or part of a structure.

110 This means that designers include:

▼ architects, civil and structural engineers, building surveyors, landscape architects, and design practices (of whatever discipline) contributing to, or having overall responsibility for, any part of the design, eg drainage engineers designing the drainage for a new development;

▼ anyone who specifies or alters a design, or who specifies the use of a particular method of work or material, eg a quantity surveyor who insists on specific material or a client who stipulates a particular layout for a new production building;

▼ building service designers, engineering practices or others designing fixed plant which people can fall more than 2 metres from (this includes ventilation and electrical systems), eg a specialist provider of permanent fire extinguishing installations;

▼ those purchasing materials where the choice has been left open, eg people purchasing building blocks and so deciding the weights that bricklayers must handle;

▼ contractors carrying out design work as part of their contribution to a project, eg an engineering contractor providing design, procurement and construction management services;

▼ temporary works engineers, including those designing formwork, falsework, scaffolding, and sheet piling;

▼ interior designers, including shop-fitters who also develop the design;

▼ anyone specifying or designing how demolition, dismantling work, structural alteration, or formation of openings, is to be carried out; and

▼ heritage organisations who specify how work is to be done in detail, eg providing detailed requirements to stabilise existing structures.

111 Local authority or government officials may provide advice relating to designs and relevant statutory requirements, eg building regulations, but this does not make them designers.

What designers must do
Regulation 13

112 Designers must:

▼ take reasonable steps to ensure that clients are aware of their duties under CDM before starting design work;

▼ prepare designs with adequate regard to health and safety, and to the information supplied by the client;

▼ provide adequate information in or with the design;

▼ co-operate with the planning supervisor and with any other designers so that each of them can comply with their duties under the Regulations. This includes providing any information needed for the health and safety file.

> ### Example 11
>
> A surveyor identified that floor tiles specified required a solvent-based adhesive. On investigation he found a similar tile that met the specification and could be fixed using a water-based adhesive. This significantly reduced the health risk.

REGULATION 13

113 Under CDM, designers must ensure that any designs they prepare for the purposes of construction work avoid risks to:

▼ anybody carrying out construction or cleaning work (see paragraph 22) in or on the structure at any time; and

▼ anyone else who may be affected by this work, for example people who work in the building, customers or the general public.

114 Designers' duties also apply to modifications to designs. These need to be properly managed. Hurriedly produced solutions to problems, or other last minute changes, can have tragic consequences if the implications are not identified and thought through.

115 Designers also have duties under other legislation. This includes section 3 of HSWA, and the Management Regulations. Compliance with regulation 13 of CDM, as set out in this section, will also ensure compliance with regulation 3(1), (2) and (6) of the Management Regulations in respect of risks to those constructing the design. Designers still need to consider the implications of Building Regulations and fire safety requirements, and any requirements that will apply to the finished structure, eg the Workplace Regulations.

116 Guidance on duties under regulation 13 of CDM is provided in this section, but designers who sub-contract design work or appoint contractors also have duties under regulations 8 and 9 regarding the competence of these designers or contractors. The section titled *Competence and resources* gives guidance on these issues.

When do these duties apply?

117 The duties of designers under CDM apply whenever they prepare a design 'for the purposes of construction work'. These purposes include obtaining estimates, bidding for grants, and obtaining tenders, as well as actual construction work. This does not depend upon the existence of a client, on funds having been allocated, on planning permission having been given, or on appointments having been made. The designer has duties even if the client is a domestic client, or if the project is not notifiable. A range of practical guidance on risk reduction for designers is available. These include *CDM Regulations - work sector guidance for designers;*[3] *CDM Regulations - case study guidance for designers: an interim report;*[4] *CDM training pack for designers;*[5] *Designing for health and safety in construction. A guide for designers on the Construction (Design and Management) Regulations 1994*[6] and *Construction (Design and Management) Regulations 1994: the role of the designer.*[7]

Making clients aware of their responsibilities
Regulation 13(1)

REGULATION 13(1)

118 Designers are often the first point of contact for a client. CDM requires them to take reasonable steps to ensure that clients are aware of their duties under the regulations. This can be achieved through meetings or by providing briefings to the client. Designers should draw the client's attention to:

▼ this book, in particular, the first three sections; and

▼ the HSC leaflet *Having construction work done? Duties of clients under the Construction (Design and Management) Regulations 1994.*[8]

119 When dealing with an inexperienced client, it is useful if the designer can emphasise the importance of:

▼ the client's role;

▼ good health and safety management; and

▼ making early appointments (see paragraphs 11 and 60 and the section titled *The client*).

Preparing a design
Regulation 13

REGULATION 13(1)

120 Designers must critically assess their design proposals at an early stage, and then throughout the design process, to ensure that health and safety issues are identified and addressed. Designers' duties under CDM are concerned with the risks to those carrying out the proposed work and others affected by it, for example people working at the structure and the public. When the design is being prepared, these risks don't yet exist. But there is a potential for harm when the construction work takes place. This potential for harm is known as a 'hazard'. A 'risk' is the likelihood of this harm being realised. The extent of the risk depends on how likely it is, how severe the harm might be, and the numbers of people at risk. The glossary at Appendix 6 sets out fuller definitions of hazard and risk.

> **Example 12**
>
> A designer initially considered the use of a water-based paint for the exterior of a metal spire on a tall building to reduce exposure to solvents. She then determined that the level of exposure to solvents from a solvent-based paint would be low, and the metalwork would require more frequent repainting with a water-based paint.
> She concluded that it was better to specify the solvent-based paint because of the high risk of working at height.

121 The first stage in reducing risk is to identify the hazards in a proposed design. The next stage is to eliminate each hazard, if feasible. It is always best to design hazards out, so that no one is put at risk, but it is counterproductive to design out one hazard, only to introduce others that would result in a higher level of risk.

122 Where it is not feasible to eliminate a hazard the next stage is to consider what can be done to reduce the risk during the construction work - this includes cleaning, maintenance or demolition. In most cases it is sufficient to approach this using experience and published guidance, without sophisticated risk analysis techniques. Designs which reduce the risks to everyone exposed should be used before turning to measures that only protect individuals - for example it is better to provide edge protection than rely on fall arrest systems.

123 Finally, designers must provide the information necessary to identify and manage the remaining risks.

REGULATION 13

124 'Standard' design solutions, for scaffolding, falsework, etc that comply with recognised codes of practice are often used. Such solutions normally meet the risk control requirements of regulation 13. However, where such solutions are adapted the designer needs to consider carefully whether the risk is still effectively controlled.

125 There is little to be gained by detailed comparison of construction techniques that present similar risks, for example whether to specify a steel frame or concrete portal building. The focus should be on issues that are known to have the potential to reduce risks significantly, including those set out later in this section.

126 Significant risks of death or serious personal injury, including to health, are not acceptable on any grounds. Designers must not produce designs that cannot be constructed safely. A team approach, taking advantage of the practical knowledge that contractors and others have, helps to make sure designs are safe to construct.

Hazards to consider in design

127 This section identifies some areas over which the designer has direct influence. The areas cover construction as well as future maintenance and cleaning requirements. This is not an exhaustive list, nor is each item relevant to every project. The designer should, where possible:

(a) select the position and design of structures to minimise risks from site hazards, including:

▼ buried services, including gas pipelines;

▼ overhead cables;

▼ traffic movements to, from and around the site;

▼ contaminated ground, for example minimising disturbance by using shallow excavations and driven, rather than bored, piles.

(b) design out health hazards, for example:

▼ specify less hazardous materials, eg solvent-free or low solvent adhesives and water-based paints;

Example 13

The original ground plan of a proposed structure was along a busy main road. This left no clear route for deliveries without a partial road closure. The design was reviewed and the footprint of the building moved by 5 metres. This improved the safety of deliveries and off-loading operations and reduced disruption to the surrounding area.

Example 14

A consultant interior designer specified the use of hardwood panelling in a prestigious office development. The drawings showing the location and fixing details for the panels were annotated to indicate the health hazards associated with hardwood dusts - asthma and nasal cancer. The contractors noted this and specified to the supplier that the panels should be formed, cut and drilled in the controlled environment of the supplier's workshop to minimise the release of hardwood dust.

▼ avoid processes that create hazardous fumes, vapours, dust, noise or vibration, including disturbance of existing asbestos, cutting chases in brickwork and concrete, breaking down cast in-situ piles to level, scabbling concrete, hand digging tunnels, flame cutting or sanding areas coated with lead paint or cadmium;

▼ specify materials that are easy to handle, eg lighter weight building blocks;

▼ design block paved areas to enable mechanical handling and laying of blocks.

(c) design out safety hazards, for example:

▼ the need for work at height, particularly where it would involve work from ladders, or where safe means of access and a safe place of work is not provided;

▼ fragile roofing materials;

▼ deep or long excavations in public areas or on highways;

▼ materials that could create a significant fire risk during construction.

(d) consider prefabrication to minimise hazardous work or to allow it to be carried out in more controlled conditions off-site including, for example:

▼ design elements, such as structural steel work and process plant, so that sub-assemblies can be erected at ground level and then safely lifted into place;

▼ arrange for cutting to size to be done off-site, under controlled conditions, to reduce the amount of dust released.

Example 15

A client wanted a glass atrium in a shopping precinct. The designer was aware of the high risk of people falling through such fragile materials, and so tried to agree a suitable alternative approach. He was unsuccessful in this and so he designed in suitable access equipment to enable safe construction, maintenance and cleaning inside and out.

Example 16

A landscaping contractor provided scaled drawings of flat garden areas which were surrounded by concrete kerb stones. This enabled the ground-work sub-contractor to calculate the number of kerb stones and arrange for all cutting to size to be done off-site under controlled conditions. This reduced the amount of silica dust released.

Example 17

A fractionation column on a catalytic cracking plant was designed so that it could be assembled horizontally at ground level, scaffolded and then lifted into a vertical position. This substantially reduced the risk of falls.

Example 18

During the construction of a multi-storey office block, the design sequence required the stairways to be installed progressively as the floors were completed. This provided much quicker and safer access for people and materials than ladders.

(e) design in features that reduce the risk of falling/injury where it is not possible to avoid work at height, for example:

▼ early installation of permanent access, such as stairs, to reduce the use of ladders;

▼ edge protection or other features that increase the safety of access and construction.

Example 19

In preparing the drainage layout for a fast track project, the drainage lines were arranged so that the drains could be laid without preventing access for the use of mobile elevating work platforms which had been chosen to provide safe access for the erection of the structural steelwork.

(f) design to simplify safe construction, for example:

▼ provide lifting points and mark the weight, and centre of gravity of heavy or awkward items requiring slinging both on drawings and on the items themselves;

▼ make allowance for temporary works required during construction;

▼ design joints in vertical structural steel members so that bolting up can easily be done by someone standing on a permanent floor, and by use of seating angles to provide support while the bolts are put in place;

▼ design connections to minimise the risk of incorrect assembly.

(g) design to simplify future maintenance and cleaning work, for example:

▼ make provision for safe permanent access;

▼ specify windows that can be cleaned from the inside;

▼ design plant rooms to allow safe access to plant and for its removal and replacement;

▼ design safe access for roof-mounted plant, and roof maintenance;

▼ make provision for safe temporary access to allow for painting and maintenance of facades, etc. This might involve allowing for access by mobile elevating work platforms or for erection of scaffolding.

(h) identify demolition hazards for inclusion in the health and safety file, for example:

▼ sources of substantial stored energy, including pre- or post-tensioned members;

▼ unusual stability concepts;

▼ alterations that have changed the structure.

128 Designers need to understand how the structure can be constructed, cleaned and maintained safely. This involves:

▼ taking full account of the risks that can arise during the proposed construction processes, giving particular attention to new or unfamiliar processes, and to those that may place large numbers of people at risk;

▼ considering the stability of partially erected structures and, where necessary, providing information to show how temporary stability could be achieved during construction;

▼ considering the effect of proposed work on the integrity of existing structures, particularly during refurbishment;

▼ ensuring that the overall design takes full account of any temporary works, for example falsework, which may be needed, no matter who is to develop those works;

▼ ensuring that there are suitable arrangements (for example access and hard standing) for cranes, and other heavy equipment, if required.

129 Occupied buildings or sites and refurbishment present special risks that can often be avoided or reduced if they are identified and addressed at the design stage. Work such as underpinning and creating openings can threaten the stability of structures by substantially weakening them or because of faults in the original construction, or subsequent work. Deciding the design strategy, timing, and sequence of the work requires good communication and co-operation between all parties.

Providing information
Regulation 13(2)(b)

REGULATION 13(2)(b)

Example 20

A designer considered using augered piles for a scheme to be built on contaminated land. He recognised that workers could be exposed to a toxic hazard. As a raft foundation was not viable from an engineering viewpoint, driven piles were specified. However, if augered piles had been the only reasonably practicable solution, the designer would have needed to include the possibility of exposure to toxic substances in information for the pre-tender health and safety plan.

130 Designers must include adequate health and safety information with the design. This includes information about hazards that remain in the design, and the resulting risks. They need to make clear to planning supervisors, or whoever is preparing the pre-tender plan, any assumptions about working methods or precautions, so that the people carrying out the construction work can take them into account.

131 Designers do not need to mention every hazard or assumption, as this can obscure the significant issues, but they do need to point out significant hazards. These are not necessarily those that result in the greatest risks, but those that are:

▼ not likely to be obvious to a competent contractor or other designers,

▼ unusual, or

▼ likely to be difficult to manage effectively.

To identify significant hazards designers must understand how the design can be built.

132 Examples of significant hazards where designers always need to provide information include:

(a) hazards that could cause multiple fatalities to the public, such as tunnelling, or the use of a crane close to a busy public place, major road or railway;

(b) **temporary works, required to ensure stability during the construction, alteration or demolition of the whole or any part of the structure, eg bracing during construction of steel or concrete frame buildings;**

(c) **hazardous or flammable substances specified in the design, eg epoxy grouts, fungicidal paints, or those containing isocyanates;**

(d) **features of the design and sequences of assembly or disassembly that are crucial to safe working;**

(e) **specific problems and possible solutions, for example arrangements to enable the removal of a large item of plant from the basement of a building;**

(f) **structures that create particular access problems, such as domed glass structures;**

(g) **heavy or awkward prefabricated elements likely to create risks in handling; and**

(h) **areas needing access where normal methods of tying scaffolds may not be feasible, such as facades that have no opening windows and cannot be drilled.**

133 Information should be clear, precise, and in a form suitable for the users. This can be achieved using, for example:

(a) **notes on drawings - these are immediately available to those carrying out the work, they can refer to other documents if more detail is needed, and be annotated to keep them up to date;**

(b) **a register, or list of significant hazards, with suggested control measures;**

(c) **suggested construction sequences showing how the design could be erected safely, where this is not obvious, for example suggested sequences for putting up stressed skin roofs. Contractors may then adopt this method or develop their own approach.**

> ### Example 21
>
> A structural engineering consultancy was engaged to provide detailed design drawings for the steelwork to be incorporated in a complex alteration to an existing structure. The company recognised that many of the structural steel elements were of different lengths and the site layout meant that it would be difficult to lift the beams into position during assembly. The structural engineer ensured that simple lifting brackets were designed into each structural steel element, and that the lifting points were marked on the design drawings. This reduced the likelihood of error on site and the time taken for installation of the steel was reduced by a third.

Co-ordination and co-operation
Regulation 13(2)(c)

REGULATION 13(2)(c)

134 Designers must co-operate with planning supervisors and with other designers, including those designing temporary works, to co-ordinate the work so that everyone can fulfil their responsibilities. This co-operation and co-ordination ensures that hazards due to incompatibilities between designs are identified and avoided as early as possible, and that the right information is provided for the pre-tender plan and health and safety file. Co-operation can be encouraged by:

▼ appointing a lead designer, where many designers are involved;

▼ agreeing a common approach to risk reduction during design;

▼ regular meetings of all the design team, contractors, and others;

▼ regular reviews of developing designs;

▼ joint meetings to review designs, where there is a shared interest in an issue; and

▼ site visits.

Design of components

135 Manufacturers supplying standardised products which can be used in any project are not designers under CDM, although they may have duties under supply legislation. The person who selects the product is the designer under CDM and must take account of health and safety issues arising from its use. If a product is purpose-made for a project, the person who prepared the specification is a designer under CDM, and so is the manufacturer who develops the detailed design.

What designers don't have to do

136 Under CDM, designers are not required to:

▼ take into account or provide information about unforeseeable hazards and risks;

▼ specify construction methods, except where the design assumes or requires a particular construction or erection sequence, or where a competent contractor might need this information;

▼ exercise any health and safety management function over contractors or others; or

▼ review and report on contractors' health and safety performance (although, like anyone else, they should point out unsafe practices that they notice to an appropriate person, such as the site manager).

137 Designers are not legally required to keep records of the process they use to reach a safe design, commonly known as the design risk assessment. However, brief records of the points considered, the conclusions reached, and the basis for those conclusions, can be very helpful when designs are passed from one designer to another. These records also enable detail designers to understand the decisions taken, and the implications for their work. If these decisions are not recorded it is more difficult and expensive to evaluate variances and design changes, and for designers to demonstrate that they have exercised reasonable professional judgement and complied with CDM.

The planning supervisor

138 The planning supervisor's main responsibility is to ensure that all those who carry out design work on a project, particularly during the design phase, collaborate and pay adequate attention to the need to reduce risk wherever possible. By doing this, planning supervisors can make a significant contribution to reducing the risks to workers during construction. Their early involvement with designers provides an opportunity to make sure that hazards are being eliminated and risks reduced.

139 CDM requires clients to appoint a planning supervisor as soon as they are in a position to judge the competence and resources needed for the proposed project. This needs to be at or before the start of design work. The planning supervisor can be an individual or an organisation, someone completely independent, or one of the other dutyholders (the client, designer or principal contractor). The planning supervisor needs a sound working knowledge of health and safety in construction work; a thorough knowledge of the design process; and experience of the site processes likely to be involved in the project and in future maintenance, refurbishment or demolition. The size and complexity of the project will determine whether an individual is capable, and has the resources, to carry out all of the work required.

140 Planning supervisors can usefully emphasise the importance of the client's role, and the benefits of good management of the project and early appointments. The leaflet *Having construction work done?*[8] may be helpful.

141 Planning supervisors need the co-operation of all the other parties involved in the project if they are to be effective in ensuring that risks are reduced. They should avoid an over-bureaucratic approach, not least because it makes it harder to gain this co-operation.

What planning supervisors must do
Regulations 7, 14 and 15

142 Planning supervisors must:
- be able to advise the client and any contractors on competence, and the adequacy of resources (including time) when they are considering appointments;
- be able to advise on the initial contents of the construction phase health and safety plan;

Example 22

The planning supervisor noted that a design required the heads of in situ cast pile caps to be broken down by hand, causing the team considerable exposure to noise and hand-arm vibration. He suggested that by slightly redesigning the reinforcing steelwork and fitting it with protective sleeving before the pour, it would be possible to use either a machine-mounted concrete crusher or a hydraulic burster instead of hand-held breakers. This suggestion was agreed with the designer and adopted, resulting in considerable time savings as well as reducing the health risk.

REGULATIONS 7, 14 & 15

▼ take reasonable steps to ensure co-operation between designers (see paragraph 134);

▼ ensure, so far as is reasonably practicable, that enough attention has been paid to health and safety during design; and that the design includes adequate information about anything which might affect the health or safety of people carrying out construction or cleaning work, or anyone else who might be affected by this work;

▼ ensure that the project is notified to HSE (see paragraphs 42-51);

▼ ensure that a pre-tender, or pre-construction, health and safety plan is prepared in good time; and

▼ ensure that a health and safety file is prepared, reviewed and amended as necessary and given to the client.

The planning supervisor and the design
Regulation 14(a) and (b)

143 Planning supervisors have to be satisfied that designs address the need to eliminate and control risks, as required by regulation 13(2). This is the case even if the designer is not available to discuss the issues. Where a number of designers are involved, planning supervisors also need to take reasonable steps to ensure co-operation between them on the health and safety implications of the designs, and to ensure that any problems are resolved (paragraph 134).

144 Planning supervisors must also ensure, so far as is reasonably practicable, that designers provide adequate information about the health and safety implications of their designs (paragraphs 130-133).

145 Planning supervisors are not necessarily designers, and they do not have to undertake any design work themselves. Planning supervisors who identify important health and safety issues that have not been addressed in a design should draw them to the attention of the designer.

146 In practice, design continues throughout a project, so the planning supervisor has a continuing role during the construction phase in ensuring that designers, including those engaged by a contractor, co-operate with each other, and meet the requirements of the regulations.

147 The design of temporary works, such as falsework, formwork and scaffolding, falls within the scope of CDM. Planning supervisors have to:
(a) take reasonable steps to ensure co-operation between permanent and temporary works designers, in particular to ensure that the design of

> ## Example 23
>
> The planning supervisor ensured that the mechanical and electrical contractor for a multi-storey office block discussed the location of the services with the pre-cast floor contractor. This allowed the service drawings to be completed in time for service voids to be pre-formed in the pre-cast floors during the manufacturing stage. This avoided extensive diamond drilling on site, reducing workers' exposure to noise.

REGULATION 14(a) & (b)

permanent works takes full account of the health and safety implications for temporary works design; and

(b) ensure, so far as is reasonably practicable, that the temporary works designer does what the regulations require of designers.

148 Planning supervisors need to pay particular attention to late changes in the design, for example revisions on architects' instructions, to ensure that they do not result in significantly increased risks.

149 Planning supervisors may need to encourage or arrange design review meetings if they are not satisfied there is sufficient interaction between designers or if adequate regard is not being given to health and safety. Such meetings can identify unforeseen problems.

Health and safety plan before construction
Regulation 15

REGULATION 15

150 Planning supervisors must ensure that a suitable health and safety plan is prepared before contractors are appointed to carry out or manage the work. This is often known as the pre-tender, pre-construction, or outline health and safety plan. Its purpose is to draw together the project-specific information obtained from the client and designer during the design and the early planning stages, so that the health and safety issues are made clear. Contractors can then take these into account when preparing an offer to the client, demonstrating their competence. The information is also useful later, when planning the construction work.

151 The planning supervisor needs to examine all the available information to identify the key health and safety issues for the plan. In particular, issues that have significant resource implications need to be clearly identified. Any client requirements which have significant implications for health and safety must be clearly stated. The section titled *The health and safety plan* provides further information.

152 Planning supervisors may request information from others to include in the plan, but usually collate, manage and issue it themselves. The plan should be issued with the tender documents, so that those tendering have all necessary information.

Advising clients and contractors
Regulation 14(c)

REGULATION 14(c)

153 The planning supervisor has to be able to advise the client on the competence and the adequacy of resources of both designers and contractors, and contractors on the competence and adequacy of resources of designers. The section titled *Competence and resources* provides more information on issues to consider. They should also be able to advise clients whether the initial construction phase health and safety plan is adequate (see section titled *The health and safety plan*).

Health and safety file
Regulation 14(d)

154 The planning supervisor must ensure that a suitable health and safety file is prepared for each structure. This requires the co-operation of several dutyholders. It is helpful if an early start is made, with everybody working together to identify the type of information that should be in the health and safety file. The planning supervisor obtains the required information from others, and in most cases also prepares the file. The section titled *The health and safety file* provides more information.

What planning supervisors don't have to do

155 Under CDM, planning supervisors are not required to:

▼ provide advice about the competence and resources of designers and contractors, unless requested;

▼ approve the appointment of designers, principal contractors or contractors;

▼ approve or check designs, although they have to be satisfied that designs address the need to eliminate and control risks;

▼ approve the principal contractor's construction phase health and safety plan, although they have to be able to advise clients on its adequacy;

▼ supervise the principal contractor's implementation of the construction phase health and safety plan; or

▼ supervise or monitor construction work.

The principal contractor

156 Good management of health and safety is crucial to the successful delivery of a construction project. The distinctive and key duty of principal contractors is the effective management of health and safety during the construction phase of a project. Principal contractors are responsible for managing and co-ordinating all construction phase health and safety issues. CDM provides a framework for this process, with the key risk management issues being set out in the construction phase health and safety plan.

Who are principal contractors?
Regulation 6(2)

REGULATION 6(2)

157 Principal contractors are usually the main or managing contractor. A principal contractor must be a contractor, that is someone who undertakes, carries out or manages construction work. Principal contractors need to satisfy prospective clients that they are competent and adequately resourced. If clients manage their own construction work and are competent to manage the project in hand they may appoint themselves.

What principal contractors must do
Regulations 15, 16, 17 & 18

REGULATIONS 15, 16, 17 & 18

> ### Example 24
>
> A large client wanted to fit out a warehouse that had been left as an empty shell. The client had long-term relationships with specialist suppliers and contractors who could carry out most of the work. Each of these was only required on site for a few days, although the work as a whole was notifiable. The client decided to act as principal contractor and planning supervisor, and appointed an experienced construction manager to plan, co-ordinate and manage the work. The client's own staff controlled access to the site.

158 Principal contractors must:
- ▼ satisfy themselves that the designers and contractors they engage are competent and adequately resourced (clients must consider these issues for designers and contractors they appoint directly). The section titled *Competence and resources* provides more information about assessing competence;
- ▼ ensure that a suitable construction phase health and safety plan (called 'the plan' in this section) is:
  - ▼ prepared before construction begins;
  - ▼ implemented; and
  - ▼ kept up to date as the project progresses;
- ▼ promote co-operation between all contractors;
- ▼ restrict entry to the site to authorised people;
- ▼ enforce any site rules;
- ▼ display the project notification on site;
- ▼ provide relevant information to contractors, including any who are self-employed. The section titled *Information and training* provides more information on how to do this;
- ▼ provide the planning supervisor promptly with any information relevant to the health and safety file. The section titled *The health and safety file* discusses the requirement for a health and safety file;

▼ encourage people at work, or their representatives, to offer advice on health and safety. This is covered in more detail in the section titled *Involving the workforce*;

▼ ensure that people at work receive information and training in health and safety; and

▼ ensure that the workforce is consulted about health and safety matters (see section titled *Involving the workforce*).

159 The principal contractor may also include reasonable rules in the plan and give reasonable directions to any contractor.

Health and safety plan in the construction phase
Regulation 15(4)

REGULATION 15(4)

160 Principal contractors must develop a suitable health and safety plan for the project. The plan provides a focus for managing and co-ordinating health and safety. The amount of detail in the plan depends on the nature and extent of the project and on the contracting arrangements for the construction work. The plan needs to explain how the key health and safety issues will be managed. It must be relevant to the particular project, and should build on the information in the pre-tender health and safety plan.

161 The plan must include information about arrangements for the welfare of workers. Under the Construction (Health, Safety and Welfare) Regulations 1996, the person in control of a construction site must ensure that welfare facilities are provided and maintained to the required standard from the outset. Where CDM applies, this responsibility normally falls to the principal contractor. Effective washing facilities are a vital part of health precautions, for example, against cement contact dermatitis and contamination by other hazardous substances.

162 The section titled *The health and safety plan* gives more information.

Implementing and monitoring the plan
Health and Safety at Work etc Act 1974, Sections 2 and 3, and CDM Regulations 15 (4)(a) and 16

HSW SECTIONS 2 & 3, AND CDM REGULATIONS 15(4)(a) & 16

163 Principal contractors must take reasonable measures to make sure the construction phase plan is implemented throughout the construction phase. This helps ensure the health and safety of their employees and others who may be affected by the work, including the public.

164 To achieve this, principal contractors need to monitor the way the work is done to ensure that the precautions described in the construction phase plan are followed in practice. Where they find that contractors are not complying with the plan, and health and safety is put at risk, principal contractors must take appropriate action to deal with the risk. The principal contractor has powers under regulation 16(2) to give reasonable directions to any contractor, and regulation 19(1)(c) requires contractors to comply.

165 Monitoring by principal contractors may show that the plan needs to be changed, for example because it has shortcomings. They should ensure that contractors are informed about any significant changes.

Communication and co-operation
Regulations 16(1)(a) and 19(1)(a)

166 Contractors must co-operate with each other so that all can comply with their legal obligations. Co-operation is essential, particularly on multi-contractor sites, if healthy and safe working conditions are to be achieved.

167 Principal contractors must actively encourage co-operation between contractors from an early stage. Practical ways to do this include regular:

(a) discussion of site health and safety issues with all contractors. This can take place before work starts, and as part of regular site meetings once work is under way. It is important that such discussions encourage contractors to monitor and review their own health and safety arrangements, rather than relying solely on the oversight of the principal contractor.

(b) review of the health and safety plan to ensure that it is relevant, practical and up to date. Principal contractors need to ensure that other contractors provide the information to enable them to do this. In turn, they need to provide information to enable contractors to manage their work safely. Such information exchanges should form part of any regular site meetings.

(c) discussion of planned work to identify where one contractor's work may adversely affect others, for example excavations beneath scaffolding, roofers working above bricklayers or demolition and most other work.

168 Good communication is essential to co-operation and risk control. Information about risks and precautions can be communicated by, for example:

(a) drawings that highlight hazards or unusual work sequences identified by

Example 25

On a busy construction site employing several contractors, the key details of the construction phase health and safety plan were transferred to a wall chart and displayed in the site office and in the canteen. This enabled all visitors and workers on site to find relevant information quickly and easily. The chart was reviewed on a weekly basis and any necessary revisions made.

Example 26

New chemical processing plant was being installed in a factory. The clients had included requirements about the safety of their workforce and plant in the pre-tender plan. The plan included details of those parts of the site the client would continue to occupy, information about the permit-to-work system, emergency procedures and traffic management arrangements. Regular meetings were held to ensure good communication and co-ordination.

designers, with clear advice on where to find more information;

(b) the relevant parts of the plan;

(c) meetings to plan and co-ordinate the work;

(d) effective arrangements to discuss the plan with those involved (section titled *Information and training*);

(e) making the plan available to workers and their representatives;

(f) induction training and toolbox talks to ensure workers understand the risks and precautions;

(g) providing a leaflet explaining the site rules that can be given to everyone at the induction training.

169 Much design work is carried out for contractors after construction work has started. Principal contractors should encourage designers working during the construction phase to discuss their proposed plans with each other at an early stage to ensure compatibility before they finalise their plans. Principal contractors should also encourage them to pass relevant information to the planning supervisor at an appropriate time.

170 Although regulations 16(1)(a) and 19(1)(a) only deal with co-operation between contractors, the same principles apply to co-operation with other parties, for example clients, designers and others affected by the work. There are general requirements regarding co-operation in the Management Regulations. Appendix 2 provides more details.

Rules
Regulation 16(1)(b) and 2(b)

REGULATION 16(1)(b) & 2(b)

171 Principal contractors may include reasonable rules for the management of construction work in the health and safety plan, which others on the site have to follow. These may cover issues such as restricted areas, permit-to-work systems and emergency plans. In some cases they are needed to reflect the requirements of clients. Any rules must be:

▼ set out in the plan in writing;

▼ understandable to those who have to follow them;

▼ brought to the attention of everyone who has to follow them; and

▼ enforced.

Controlling access onto sites
Regulation 16(1)(c)

REGULATION 16(1)(c)

172 A principal contractor must take reasonable measures to ensure that no unauthorised person enters the work area. Only people who are explicitly authorised, individually or collectively, by the principal contractor, should be allowed

Example 27

A site compound was set up near the site entrance. This meant that everyone going in or out had to pass through the welfare facilities, where a register was kept listing every person who entered or left the site.

access to the site. The authorisation may cover the whole site or be restricted to certain areas. HSE Inspectors, and others who have statutory powers to enter the site, should be treated as authorised people. Authorised people should have relevant site rules explained to them and undertake any necessary induction training. Some authorised visitors may need to be supervised while on site or visiting specific areas.

173 How access is controlled depends on the nature of the project, the risks and location. The boundaries of all sites should be physically defined, where practical, by suitable barriers.[a] The type of barriers should reflect the nature of the site and its surroundings. Special consideration is needed where:

▼ rights of way cross sites;

▼ sites are in, or next to, other work areas;

▼ new houses are being built on a development where some houses are already occupied; or

▼ there are children and other vulnerable people nearby.

174 The effectiveness of the arrangements needs to be reviewed in the light of experience. In particular, their adequacy should be carefully reviewed if there is evidence of children playing on, or near the site.

(a) *Protecting the public: Your next move*[9] provides further information about site security.

Display of notification to HSE
Regulation 16(1)(d)

REGULATION 16(1)(d)

175 A legible copy of the most up-to-date information notified to HSE must be clearly displayed on site by the principal contractor, where it can be read by people working on the site and affected by it. The principal contractor needs to ensure that all contractors are aware of the contents of the notice.

Training and information
Regulation 17

REGULATION 17

176 Training is vital to securing health and safety on site. The principal contractor has to ensure that contractors provide their employees with information about the risks to their health and safety, the precautions required and with adequate training about new or increased risks arising from their work on the project. The section titled *Information and training* gives further guidance. Appendix 2 reproduces relevant parts of the Management Regulations 1999.

Example 28

In addition to a site-specific safety induction, every worker who entered the site was provided with a small pocket card detailing the site health and safety rules. Any new rules introduced as a result of work being carried out on the site were clearly displayed at the site entrance and the cards were reprinted and re-issued.

How many principal contractors can there be?

177 There can only be one principal contractor for a project at any one time. Sometimes two or more projects take place on a site at the same time. This can happen if different clients commission adjacent work, or if a client procures two unrelated packages of work. In CDM terms there is more than one project on site only if the packages of work are truly independent and do not rely upon one another for their viability or completion.

178 Where overlapping projects are running on a single construction site, it is best to appoint one principal contractor for them all. If this is not done, the health and safety plans of all the principal contractors should take account of any interfaces between their work and the other projects. The requirements of regulations 8, 9 and 11 of the Management Regulations (see Appendix 2) are also relevant.

Example 29

A principal contractor was awarded a contract to build a retail park. The individual units were handed over to the tenants on practical completion of the unit. The tenants then appointed their own principal contractors to fit out the units as separate projects.

The tenants were informed of the need to liaise with the principal contractor for the retail park, where necessary complying with its health and safety plan.

Contractors

179 Each year many people die in accidents and even more suffer ill health as a result of inadequate attention to health and safety during construction work. Contractors and their employees - those actually doing the construction work - are most at risk of injury and ill health. They have a key role to play, in co-operation with the principal contractor, in managing the work to ensure health and safety.

180 All contractors (including utilities, specialist contractors, contractors nominated by the client and the self-employed) have a part to play in ensuring that the site is a safe place to work. The key to this is communication and co-operation between all those involved. In addition to their duties under CDM, it is important that contractors understand and comply with other relevant health and safety law. Some of the most relevant requirements are listed in the *Further information* section at the end of this book.

Contractors and the self-employed

181 Most of CDM covers both employees and the self-employed (many of whom will also be contractors) without distinction. People working under the control of others are usually their employees for health and safety purposes, even if they are treated as self-employed for tax and national insurance. Section 3 of HSWA and CHSWR also create duties towards the self-employed, and place duties on them.

What contractors must do

Regulations 7(5), (6), 8 (2), (3), 9 (2), (3) and 19

REGULATIONS 7(5), (6), 8(2), (3), 9(2), (3) & 19

182 All contractors must:
▼ satisfy themselves that any contractors or designers they engage are competent and adequately resourced (see section titled *Competence and resources*);
▼ co-operate with the principal contractor;
▼ provide information to the principal contractor about risks to others created by their work. This information might, for example, come from risk assessments and method statements;
▼ comply with any reasonable directions from the principal contractor, and with any relevant rules in the health and safety plan;
▼ tell the principal contractor about accidents and dangerous occurrences;
▼ provide information for the health and safety file (see section titled *The health and safety file*);
▼ ensure that projects for domestic clients are notified to HSE in good time; and
▼ provide information and training to their employees (see section titled *Information and training*).

Information

Regulation 19(2), (3) and (4)

REGULATIONS 19(2), (3) & (4)

183 Contractors must not start work on a construction site, or allow their employees to start work, until they have been provided with basic information. This information must include the names of the planning supervisor and principal contractor, and the relevant parts of the health and safety plan.

184 Contractors must promptly provide the principal contractor with any information which might affect the health and safety of workers or members of the public. This includes anything which might justify a review or update of the health and safety plan. This information might come, for example, from risk assessments which contractors carry out under the Management Regulations and COSHH.

Complying with the plan

Health and Safety at Work etc Act Sections 2 and 3, and CDM Regulation 19

HSW SECTIONS 2 & 3, AND CDM REGULATION 19

185 Contractors must comply with relevant parts of the construction phase plan. This will help ensure, so far as is reasonably practicable, the health and safety of their employees and others who may be affected by their work, including the public.

186 To achieve this, contractors need to monitor the way in which they carry out their work to ensure that the health and safety precautions described in the plan are followed in practice. Where contractors find that their employees, or self-employed people that they are supervising, are not complying with the plan, they must take appropriate action to ensure health and safety.

187 Such monitoring may identify shortcomings in the plan. Where this is the case, the contractor should ensure that the principal contractor is told.

Notification of project

Regulation 7(5)

REGULATION 7(5)

188 Planning supervisors normally notify construction projects to HSE, but if contractors carry out notifiable work directly for a domestic client then they must notify HSE. Where several contractors are working together on this type of project, one of them can notify HSE on behalf of the others.

Reporting incidents

189 The Reporting of Injuries, Diseases and Dangerous Occurrences Regulations 1995 (RIDDOR) require the 'responsible person' to notify any death, reportable injury, disease or dangerous occurrence to the relevant enforcing authority. The responsible person is the employer or, for the self-employed, the principal contractor.

Regulation 19(1)(e)

REGULATION 19(1)(e)

190 Contractors must provide full information about RIDDOR incidents to principal contractors so that they can monitor compliance with health and safety law and, if necessary, review the arrangements for the management of health and safety. The health and safety plan should cover reporting of 'near miss' incidents and incident investigation.

Competence and resources

191 This section deals with assessing the competence and resources of CDM dutyholders - planning supervisors, designers, principal contractors and other contractors. Any assessment of suitability needs to take account of the role under CDM of the person or organisation. Details can be found in the respective sections and are summarised in the section titled *The client.*

192 It is in everyone's interest to ensure that those with duties under CDM are competent and adequately resourced to manage risks and avoid delays. To be competent, an organisation or individual needs to have sufficient experience, knowledge and other skills to carry out their duties satisfactorily. This includes management skills. While checking on quality, financial viability, etc, little additional effort is required to ensure that the organisation or individual is also competent and has sufficient resources to carry out their work safely. Dealing with all of these issues together is likely to work best. Assessments should focus on the needs of the particular project and be proportionate to the risks, size and complexity of the work.

What you must do
Regulations 4, 8 and 9

REGULATIONS 4, 8 & 9

193 All those with duties under CDM must satisfy themselves that those they engage or appoint are competent and have sufficient resources. This means taking reasonable steps to make sure that the organisation or individual is competent to do the relevant work and can allocate adequate resources to it. This includes making reasonable enquiries or seeking advice where necessary (regulation 2(5)(a)).

194 Planning supervisors must be in a position to advise clients about the competence of designers and contractors, and advise contractors about designers, if asked. Clients should ask for advice, unless they know enough to make the assessments themselves.

Principles
195 Assessments of competence and resources need to take place before appointments are made. The following principles underpin these assessments:
- the competence and resource requirements under CDM relate only to health and safety purposes;
- the judgement is about the dutyholder's ability to comply with their legal duties for health and safety;
- the checks carried out are for the project being planned, and should be proportionate and well-targeted;
- there is no need to repeat checks where relevant evidence exists following recent, similar work;
- in most cases, demonstration of a successful track record in similar work should be sufficient indication; and
- for simple, low-risk projects, minimal checks are needed.

196 Unnecessary bureaucracy obscures the real issues and diverts effort from them. It can result in insufficient attention being paid to the availability of adequate resources, particularly time. Standard, generic pre-qualification questionnaires have been widely used but can often be irrelevant, create a great deal of paperwork, and be of little benefit to health and safety. Moreover, they frequently tend to measure negative rather than positive issues. There are generally more positive ways to assess competence and resources, for example, site visits and one-to-one interviews can make it easier to reach a final decision.

197 It may be that the best individual or organisation is weak in certain areas. This can sometimes be addressed by putting arrangements in place to cover these weak points or by employing people with particular expertise for relevant parts of the contract.

How to assess competence and resources

198 Enquiries to assess competence and resources might usefully cover some or all of the following:

▼ information about track record: simple evidence of performance, such as personal experience from previous projects, references from those who have engaged the dutyholder on previous projects, information from reviews following previous projects, and evidence from site visits;

▼ evidence of competence of individuals on the project, including managers and supervisors. For example, this could include their practical experience and knowledge of the work; qualifications; membership of a relevant trade or professional body; and training in health and safety;

▼ the availability of sufficient, appropriate, competent people and essential equipment, facilities and management systems;

▼ whether organisations and key people can devote sufficient time to the project; and

▼ information about past health and safety performance, including previous enforcement action and the steps taken to put things right. However, an absence of enforcement action is not, on its own, a reliable indicator of competence.

199 Bids from prospective appointees should also indicate competence in the way they set out how they propose to deal with the health and safety matters identified in the pre-tender plan.

> ### Example 30
>
> A client was committed to securing high standards of health and safety during the construction phase of a major city centre redevelopment project. They set aside a sum of money to fund an occupational health professional to be present on site throughout that phase. The occupational health professional was able to carry out audiometry and checks for solvent and cement dermatitis; give training and advice on lifting and manual handling; and provide advice to contractors on reducing noise, dust and vibration hazards.

Time and resources

200 Resources is a general term which includes the necessary plant, machinery, technical facilities, trained and competent people, and time in which to discharge duties. A breakdown of funds devoted to health and safety is not required, but it may be helpful in relation to some high-risk matters specifically identified in the health and safety plan. Any check on the resources for a project involves considering the time required to carry out the design, and to draw up and develop the pre-tender and construction phase health and safety plans. The principal contractor also needs sufficient time to mobilise the labour force and equipment, arrange welfare facilities, plan and prepare for the project and carry out the construction work safely. Clearly, clients need to allocate sufficient funds to the overall project for it to be adequately resourced. It is better to have a realistic completion date than an unrealistic deadline.

Example 31

On the recommendation of a friend, a client appointed a contractor to demolish a four-storey building before work could start on a new-build project. The client was keen to get the work started quickly, and did not carry out the necessary checks on competence and resources prior to making the appointment. The contractor began work on the site almost immediately, but the building collapsed into the street causing damage to cars and adjacent properties, and closing off the road for several days. The project was delayed for many months whilst insurers debated who should pay the costs incurred by the neighbours, the emergency services, the local authority and the owners of damaged vehicles. The demolition contractor's prior experience was limited to the demolition of domestic housing.

Example 32

A principal contractor engaged a roofing company that they had worked with before to carry out refurbishment work on the roof of an existing warehouse. Competence checks were made, and these were cross-referenced with the performance of the roofing firm on the previous contracts. The contract was awarded, but the roofing firm sub-let the work to another company at a considerably reduced price. The company which carried out the work had never done such a large job before and was not competent to do the job.
A worker from this company fell to his death from the roof. The principal contractor and the roofing firm were each prosecuted for failing to adequately check the competence of the company which actually carried out the work.

Information and training

201 Good information and training on health and safety are vital. People are more likely to adopt safe working practices if they understand the reasons behind them. Effective information and training contributes positively to the health and safety culture. It is needed at all levels, from the top down, and for all disciplines. The requirements in CDM for information and training are quite limited and are placed on principal contractors. More general requirements for information and training are in CHSWR as well as across-the-board health and safety legislation like the Management Regulations.

What you must do
Regulation 17

REGULATION 17

202 Regulation 17(1) requires principal contractors to provide all contractors with information about the particular risks that they can expect to face when working on the site. This includes risks that are discovered or arise through changes to the design, the works or the site environment during the project. This information enables contractors to take account of the risks, particularly when planning and managing their work. The relevant parts of the construction phase health and safety plan, updated as necessary, should normally provide this information. The information provided must be easy for contractors to understand.

203 Under regulation 17(2), principal contractors must also make sure that contractors provide their employees with the information and training required by regulation 13(2)(b) of the Management Regulations (reproduced at Appendix 2). This is to cover new or increased risks, such as those arising from a change of responsibilities, new technology or new systems of work.

Induction
Regulation 17

REGULATION 17

Example 33

All new employees on a large transport infrastructure project attended an induction session, in works time, on their first day. Employer and trade union representatives jointly explained the key issues. The joint approach reinforced the messages and made the induction more effective.

204 To ensure people have relevant information and training for their work, principal contractors need to ensure adequate induction for all who are new to a site; this is particularly important for young workers and those who are new to the industry. Induction is not intended to provide the general health and safety information and training that people need as part of their job. This should be provided in other ways.

205 Induction should include explanation of the following:
(a) senior management commitment to health and safety;
(b) the outline of the project;

(c) the individual's immediate line manager and any other key personnel;

(d) any site-specific health and safety risks, for example in relation to access, transport, site contamination, hazardous substances and manual handling;

(e) control measures on the site, including

- any site rules laid down by the principal contractor or client, such as authorisation of mobile plant operators and scaffolders;
- any permit-to-work systems on the site;
- traffic routes;
- security arrangements;
- hearing protection zones;
- arrangements for personal protective equipment, including what is needed, where to find it and how to use it;

(f) arrangements for housekeeping and materials storage;

(g) facilities available, including welfare facilities;

(h) emergency procedures, including fire precautions, the action to take in the event of a fire, escape routes, assembly points, responsible people and the safe use of any fire fighting equipment;

(i) arrangements for first aid;

(j) arrangements for reporting accidents and other incidents;

(k) additional training planned, such as 'toolbox' talks;

(l) arrangements for workforce representation and consultation, including the identity and role of any:

- appointed trade union safety representatives,
- representatives of employee safety,
- safety committees,
- and other arrangements so that anyone working on the project can discuss and offer advice on health and safety to the principal contractor;

(m) information about the individual's responsibilities for health and safety.

General health and safety training
Construction (Health Safety and Welfare) Regulations regulation 28 and the Management Regulations regulation 13(2)

**REGULATION 28 &
MANAGEMENT
REGULATION 13(2)**

206 The limited requirements for training in CDM do not replace the wider ones in general health and safety law. These still apply. These include a requirement in the Management Regulations for new employees to be given adequate health and safety training on being recruited. Training is required for people at all levels, including managers, supervisors and site workers.

207 There are times when people need extra training or knowledge to reduce the risk of injury during particular work. This is also dealt with by the Management Regulations. These require adequate training for employees to cover new or increased risks, for example when they transfer to a new site or when a new process or item of equipment is introduced. These regulations apply to all employers involved in construction projects, including the client, planning supervisor and designer. Under CDM, principal contractors must ensure, so far as is reasonably practicable, that the employees of contractors carrying out the construction work are provided with this extra training.

208 Regulation 28 of CHSWR places a training duty on anyone in control of the way construction work is carried out. They have to ensure that workers have the training, knowledge or experience needed to minimise the risk of injury, or are suitably supervised by someone with that training, knowledge or experience. Of course, under section 2 of HSWA, even fully trained employees must still be adequately supervised.

209 When developing training schemes, it is important to ensure that the content and style are appropriate. This includes providing training in a form that trainees can understand. Workforce or trade union-appointed safety representatives can make a significant contribution to developing this training, and a joint approach can help ensure people adopt good practices.

Information
Regulation 17 and the Management Regulations

210 Under regulation 17(2) of CDM principal contractors must ensure, as far as possible, that contractors have provided their employees with information about:
▼ risks to their health and safety, including those associated with the work of other contractors (regulation 10 of the Management Regulations);
▼ precautions to control the risks (regulation 10 of the Management Regulations);
▼ emergency procedures (regulation 8 the of Management Regulations); and
▼ relevant health and safety training (regulation 13 of the Management Regulations).

211 Regulation 10 of the Management Regulations requires employers to provide their employees with understandable and relevant information on risks to their health and safety, and on precautions. It is reproduced in Appendix 2. The information should be pitched appropriately, according to the level of training, knowledge and experience of the employee.

212 Information should be provided in a way that takes account of any language difficulties or disabilities. It can be provided in whatever form is most suitable in the circumstances, as long as it can be understood by everyone. For employees with little or no understanding of spoken or written English, employers may need to make special arrangements. These could include providing translation, using interpreters, or replacing written notices with clear symbols or diagrams.

213 The construction phase health and safety plan is a valuable source of information to contractors about risks to their employees and others under their control. It needs to be kept up to date. It should include the arrangements for providing induction information and training to people on site.

REGULATION 17 & MANAGEMENT REGULATIONS

Involving the workforce

214 It is essential that the workforce and their representatives are fully involved in health and safety issues at all relevant stages of a project, particularly the construction phase. This is because the workforce are the people most at risk of injury, and because they have a lot to contribute to improving health and safety. Their first-hand involvement in the actual conditions of work means that they are often the first to identify potential problems. The workforce includes anyone at work on the site, such as members of the design team.

215 Worker representatives have an important part to play in explaining and selling safety measures to the workforce and in communicating their needs and views. On large sites, an active safety committee can be a highly effective way of encouraging the whole workforce to co-operate and participate in improving standards of health and safety. For example, committees can address common problems, review accidents and near misses, and consider how to address risks. For any committee to be successful, it must be seen by all parties to be effective. Thought must also be given as to how to involve the workforce in urgent matters, when use of a committee is not appropriate.

216 Involving the entire workforce in identifying and controlling risks is crucial to reducing the high accident rate associated with construction. Participation will be most effective when the workforce has sufficient knowledge and confidence to provide feedback, and can identify risks and explain their importance. People have the confidence to do this when they are properly trained (see section titled *Information and training*), know how to report their concerns, and see prompt action being taken as a result.

What CDM requires
217 Under regulation 18 of CDM, the principal contractor must ensure that:
▼ everyone working on the site can discuss and offer advice on matters that are liable to affect their health and safety; and
▼ there are arrangements for co-ordinating the views of employees, or their representatives, on health and safety for that site.

Involving the workforce
Regulation 18

218 There are two types of worker representative:
▼ those appointed by recognised trades unions under the Safety Representatives and Safety Committees Regulations 1977 (SRSCR); and
▼ representatives of employee safety appointed under the Health and Safety (Consultation with Employees) Regulations 1996 (HSCER).

219 Further information on SRSCR and HSCER is contained in the ACoP and guidance[10, 11] published by HSC/E.

220 Both types of representative are entitled to training that will enable them to play a full and active part in securing health and safety. Suitable training is available through a number of bodies, including trade unions.

221 Where representatives have not been appointed or do not provide complete coverage, the principal contractor must make other arrangements so that those not represented, including the self-employed, have similar opportunities to discuss health and safety issues. Arrangements should be tailored according to the size and nature of the project and risks involved.

222 Involvement is essential to good communication and the development of a safety culture. It does not depend on the use of representatives and safety committees alone. A combination of several approaches is likely to be most effective. For example:

▼ involving people actively in managing the hazards associated with their work to help identify optimum solutions and avoid expensive mistakes;

▼ informal discussions, invitations to attend open meetings and meetings with subcontractors;

▼ 'toolbox talks', which provide an opportunity for individuals to voice their concerns and become involved in health and safety issues relating to their immediate working area and tasks.

223 Clearly, highlighting the results and benefits of raising issues will encourage people to be involved.

224 Once established, the arrangements for involvement and consultation should be included in the construction phase health and safety plan. The workforce and their representatives are likely to be able to contribute to the development of this plan; and, in particular, to provide insights into specialised areas of activity. The section titled *The health and safety plan* provides more details on the plan.

225 Where there are safety representatives, representatives of employee safety, or safety committees, at a site principal contractors should use them to ensure that they are able to benefit from the experience of the workforce.

What the workforce have to do
226 By actively encouraging workforce involvement, principal contractors make it easier for individual workers to participate in, and discharge their own responsibilities for, health and safety. Under HSWA, the Management Regulations and CHSWR, workers at all levels have duties to:

▼ take reasonable care for their own health and safety and that of others who may be affected by what they do at work;

▼ co-operate with their employer in order to comply with any relevant health and safety law;

▼ report any work situation, defects or shortcomings in health and safety arrangements which might endanger themselves or others; and

▼ use all work items and method statements provided by their employer correctly, in accordance with their training and the instructions they have received.

227 Under the Management Regulations, anyone who is exposed to serious, imminent and unavoidable danger has the right to stop work and immediately proceed to a place of safety.

228 The duties placed on employees do not reduce the legal responsibilities of the employer. In particular, employers need to ensure that employees receive adequate instruction and training to enable them to comply with their duties. The section titled *Information and training* contains more information on this.

The health and safety plan

229 Regulation 15 requires a health and safety plan to be prepared and maintained until the end of the construction phase. The health and safety plan is developed in two stages: a pre-tender, also known as the pre-construction or outline plan, and a construction phase plan. These serve separate purposes, although both have the common goal of ensuring the health and safety of those involved in the project.

230 The health and safety plan at the pre-tender stage must be project-specific and address the key health and safety issues, in particular those that contractors could not reasonably be expected to identify. Its purpose is to ensure that these can be taken into account when preparing a tender or bid to the client.

231 In the construction phase, the health and safety plan builds on the information contained in the pre-tender plan and sets out arrangements for managing the project (including monitoring), taking account of the particular risks. It must also include details of arrangements for welfare facilities. The construction phase plan usually needs to be developed as the work progresses, providing a focus for the management and co-ordination of health and safety.

232 The planning supervisor needs to examine all the available information to identify the key health and safety issues for the pre-tender plan. In particular, issues that have significant resource implications need to be clearly identified, along with any other information the principal contractor is likely to need to plan the work.

Health and safety plan before construction
Regulation 15(3)

233 Planning supervisors must ensure that a suitable plan is prepared before contractors are appointed to carry out or manage the work. This pre-tender stage of the plan draws together the project-specific information obtained from the client, designer and planning supervisor during the design and early planning stages. Its purpose is to ensure that the health and safety issues are clearly identified. This allows contractors to take account of them when preparing to bid for work and later, if successful, when preparing to carry out construction work.

> **Example 34**
>
> A row of single-storey brick-built garages was to be demolished. The site was to be completely fenced off. The pre-tender health and safety plan stated that there were no services to the garages. It provided details of the access route to the garages and stated that in recent months children had been playing in the area. No other information was necessary as the contractor selected was a competent demolition contractor.

REGULATION 15(3)

234 In many cases there is no tender process. This might happen, for example, where there is only one contractor, who has already been appointed, or in design-and-build contracting, management contracting and construction management. In these circumstances a plan is still needed when initial arrangements for construction work are made, so that the contractor knows about the key health and safety issues. The plan should be developed in discussion with the principal contractor, so that the construction phase health and safety plan can take account of the relevant issues, and is available before the start of the construction phase.

235 The planning supervisor may request information from others for inclusion in the pre-tender plan, and usually collates and manages the pre-tender plan, arranging for it to be issued with the tender documents.

236 At the pre-tender stage the plan should include general information about the project, including a brief description and details of the programme. The detail needed in the plan varies according to the complexity of the project and the hazards involved. For example, little information is required for a straightforward project, such as a small warehouse on a single plot. On the other hand, a contract to build a control complex on the site of an oil refinery may require a great deal of information.

237 The aim of the pre-tender plan is to identify and target the key project specific issues, while avoiding unnecessary bureaucracy. It does not need to cover hazards that should be apparent to the competent contractor. Including information on every hazard can obscure the significant ones. However, hazards that could cause multiple fatalities to the public, such as tunnelling, or the use of a crane that could topple onto a busy public place, major road or railway, must always be considered.

238 A suitable pre-tender plan provides a focus for the management and co-ordination of health and safety. It should include information on:
(a) any stipulations from the client, for example on:
  ▼ **safety goals,**
  ▼ **management arrangements,**
  ▼ **liaison arrangements;**
(b) significant constraints or other hazards arising from the existing site or neighbourhood for example asbestos, or contaminated land;
(c) significant hazards which the designer was not able to avoid, and the precautions suggested for dealing with them;
(d) significant assumptions made by the designer about work methods, sequences and the related precautions.

239 Appendix 3 provides a more detailed list of topics that need to be addressed when preparing the pre-tender plan. The pre-tender plan can form part of other documents, for example the specification, providing the relevant health and safety issues are fully covered.

Health and safety plan in the construction phase
Regulation 15(4)

240 Under regulation 3 of the Management Regulations, the principal contractor and other contractors must identify the hazards and assess the risks related to their work, including the risks they may create for others. Using this information, and applying the principles of prevention set out in Appendix 2, the principal contractor must develop a plan suitable for the construction phase. This provides an integrated approach to the management of health and safety.

241 At this stage, the plan must set out the health and safety goals for the project and explain how the key health and safety issues will be managed. It should build on the information in the pre-tender health and safety plan. To provide a basis for safe construction, the plan must clearly explain the action needed to control key risks and must provide details of good working practice. The plan also needs to incorporate, or refer to, any required method statements, safety rules and monitoring arrangements.

242 The amount of detail needed in the plan depends on the nature and extent of the project and the contracting arrangements for the construction work. It must be relevant to the particular project. The construction phase plan should be clear in its purpose, well structured, relevant and easy for contractors and others to understand. The level of detail should be proportionate to the risks associated with the project. It should not include irrelevant material. A short, focused plan is preferable to an unnecessarily long one with limited practical use.

243 As a minimum the plan should include the following information from the start of the construction phase:
(a) general information about the project, including a brief description and details of the programme;
(b) specific procedures and arrangements for the early work;
(c) general procedures and arrangements which apply to the whole construction phase, including those for the management and monitoring of health and safety;
(d) welfare arrangements;
(e) emergency procedures; and
(f) arrangements for communication.

244 Where the design and preparation for later work is not complete at the start of the construction phase, the parts of the plan relating to that work need to be developed as information becomes available.

245 A more detailed list of topics that need to be addressed when developing the construction phase plan is included at Appendix 3. Where the principal

contractor has other documents setting out health and safety arrangements which deal with any of these issues, the construction phase plan may refer to them; they do not have to be reproduced in the document.

Implementing and monitoring the plan

246 A plan is no use if it is treated merely as a paper exercise and gathers dust. To improve standards, it must be a practical aid to the management of health and safety on site. Principal contractors and other contractors have a particular role in both implementing and monitoring the plan to ensure that it works in practice. Further information about this is given in paragraphs 163 and 185.

247 If the plan is not being followed, and health and safety is put at risk, those involved must take appropriate action to deal with the risk. Monitoring may show the plan has shortcomings and needs to be modified. Any significant changes in the plan should be brought to the attention of all those affected.

The health and safety file

248 The health and safety file provides information needed during future construction work, which includes cleaning, maintenance, alterations, refurbishment and demolition. Information in the file is essential to those doing the work. It alerts them to risks and helps them to decide how to work safely. It can also provide information for future health and safety plans and is useful to:

▼ clients, who have a duty to provide information about their premises;

▼ designers and planning supervisors during the development of further designs;

▼ those preparing pre-tender health and safety plans for future work; and

▼ principal contractors and contractors preparing to carry out or manage this work.

249 The health and safety file can provide significant benefits to the client by minimising the cost of future work. It is a key part of the information that the client, or the client's successor, is required to provide for future projects under regulation 11 (see paragraphs 83-86). So it is well worth the effort to ensure it is kept up to date after any relevant work.

250 The file is not a maintenance manual, but it can be incorporated with one, providing that this does not result in the health and safety information being lost. It does not need to stand alone, but may refer to other documentation to avoid duplication. Clients, designers, principal contractors, other contractors and planning supervisors all have legal duties in respect of the health and safety file.

What you must do
Regulations 12, 13, 14 & 16

251 In relation to the health and safety file:

▼ **planning supervisors** must ensure that a file is prepared, reviewed, amended or added to, as necessary, and given to the client;

▼ **clients, designers, principal contractors and other contractors** must supply information for the file;

▼ **clients** must take reasonable steps to ensure that the project health and safety file is kept available for future construction work; and

▼ **everyone** providing information for the health and safety file should make sure that it is accurate, and provided promptly.

252 It is important to establish at an early stage who is to compile the file. This is often the planning supervisor. In other cases, for example design-and-build contracts, the principal contractor may obtain information for the file from the specialist contractors, assemble it and give it to the planning supervisor.

253 The collection and compilation of the relevant data needs to be managed properly. It can be difficult to obtain information for the file after designers or contractors have completed their work, so it is important that the information needs are clearly spelled out in advance, for example in contracts. This will ensure that the information is prepared and handed over in the required form at an appropriate time (see paragraph 66).

The content of the file
Regulations 13(2)(b) and 14(d)

254 The file must include adequate information for anyone planning or carrying out construction or cleaning work. Information in other documents does not need to be repeated, but relevant cross-references should be included. The health and safety issues should not be obscured by the inclusion of other information which may be irrelevant. The NHBC Home Owners Information Package[12] provides suitable information for developers to give to householders.

255 A health and safety file must be produced for all CDM projects. For some projects, for example re-decoration using non-toxic materials, or simple maintenance, there may be nothing of substance to record. All that is needed in these circumstances is a very brief record of what was done, with any information that may have significance for health and safety in future work. CDM applies to all demolition work, but there is no point recording information about structures, or parts of structures, that no longer exist. However, the implications for remaining or future structures, if any, should be addressed. It may be preferable to amend or add to an existing file rather than to create a new one, depending on what will be the most useful in future work.

256 Appendix 4 sets out the topics to be considered when preparing the health and safety file. The file does not need to include the following:
▼ the pre-tender, or construction phase health and safety plan;
▼ construction phase risk assessments, method statements and COSHH assessments;
▼ details about the operation of the completed structure;
▼ construction phase accident statistics;
▼ the names and addresses of contractors and designers involved in the project; or
▼ contractual documents.

257 Some of these items may be useful to the client for later work, or may be needed for purposes apart from CDM. They may even include details that are relevant to the health and safety file, but CDM does not require the full documents to be included in the file. In fact, including such material may hide crucial information about risks.

258 CDM does not specify a format for the file. This may vary depending on the circumstances. Clients usually know how a completed project is to be managed so they should discuss the format with the planning supervisor at the start of a project and make clear their needs regarding scope, structure format and medium. Whatever its format, it should be easy to find information in the file. It may be kept electronically (with suitable backup arrangements), on paper, on film, or other durable media.

The preparation of the file

Planning supervisors
Regulation 14(d), (e) and (f)

259 Planning supervisors need to:
(a) agree the structure and format of the file, as well as who is to prepare it, with the client at the start of the project;
(b) gather relevant information throughout the project;
(c) ensure that the file is prepared;
(d) ensure that all the information required by regulation 14(d) is provided;
(e) review the file with the client to ensure they understand its purpose and value;
(f) amend or add to the file if necessary; and
(g) ensure that the file is given to the client at the end of the construction phase. Where another project, for example fitting out, begins before the end of the first project, the client may need the file earlier.

260 Planning supervisors have to ensure that a file is prepared for each structure involved in a project. However, a single file may be prepared for an entire project, provided that the user is able to find relevant information for each structure easily, including any differences between structures.

Designers
Regulation 13(2)(c)

261 Designers need to provide the person preparing the health and safety file with information for the file. They must not wait until the end of the project. The details they provide should include information of the type described in paragraph 130 ff.

Contractors
Regulation 16(1)(e)

262 Principal contractors and other contractors have to promptly provide relevant information for the file, this includes information which comes to light during work, even if it is not relevant to the work being carried out at the time. Information should be made available as early as possible to ensure the file can be:

Example 35

A pharmaceutical company decided to commission a new process plant itself and instructed the planning supervisor to provide the health and safety file on mechanical completion. At the commissioning stage the client then appointed itself as planning supervisor and principal contractor. The health and safety file was updated to include relevant commissioning information.

Example 35

A client included the preparation of the health and safety file in the planning supervisor's contract. The planning supervisor received information from the principal contractor and designers for inclusion in the health and safety file. The planning supervisor reviewed all the information provided and extracted what was needed for inclusion in the health and safety file. One contractor had provided his risk assessments. The planning supervisor did not include these because they were not relevant to future construction or cleaning work.

REGULATION 14(d), (e) & (f)

REGULATION 13(2)(c)

REGULATION 16(1)(e)

▼ developed as the project progresses; and
▼ completed in good time and handed over when the client takes over responsibility for the structure.

Clients
Regulations 11 and 12

REGULATIONS 11 & 12

263 Clients have to keep the health and safety file available for inspection by anybody who needs the information. Emergency maintenance contractors may need to see the file in advance, so that they can work safely if they are called in. To be useful, the file needs to be kept up to date and retained for as long as it is relevant.

264 If clients dispose of their entire interest in a structure, they should pass the file to the new owner and ensure that the new owner is aware of the nature and purpose of the file. If they sell part of a structure, any relevant information in the file should be passed or copied to the new owner.

265 If the client leases out all or part of the structure, arrangements need to be made for the health and safety file to be made available to the leaseholder. In some cases, the client might transfer the file to the leaseholder during the lease period. In other cases, it may be better for the client to keep the file, but tell the leaseholder that it is available. If the leaseholder acts as a client for future construction projects, the leaseholder and the original client will need to make arrangements for the file to be made available to the new planning supervisor.

266 In multi-occupancy situations, for example where a housing association owns a block of flats, the owner should keep and maintain the file, but ensure that individual flat occupiers are supplied with health and safety information concerning their home.

267 A development may include roads and sewers that will be adopted by the local authority or water company. It is generally best to treat these as separate structures and to prepare separate files.

Appendix 1

THE CONSTRUCTION (DESIGN AND MANAGEMENT) REGULATIONS 1994
As amended by the Management of Health and Safety at Work Regulations 1999 and the Construction (Design and Management)(Amendment) Regulations 2000 (modified text is shown <u>underlined</u>, deleted text is shown ~~crossed out~~).

Regulation 1   **Citation and commencement**

These Regulations may be cited as the Construction (Design and Management) Regulations 1994 and shall come into force on 31st March 1995.

Regulation 2   **Interpretation**

(1) In these Regulations, unless the context otherwise requires -

"agent" in relation to any client means any person who acts as agent for a client in connection with the carrying on by the person of a trade, business or other undertaking (whether for profit or not);

"cleaning work" means the cleaning of any window or any transparent or translucent wall, ceiling or roof in or on a structure where such cleaning involves a risk of a person falling more than 2 metres;

"client" means any person for whom a project is carried out, whether it is carried out by another person or is carried out in-house;

"construction phase" means the period of time starting when construction work in any project starts and ending when construction work in that project is completed;

"construction work" means the carrying out of any building, civil engineering or engineering construction work and includes any of the following -

(a) the construction, alteration, conversion, fitting out, commissioning, renovation, repair, upkeep, redecoration or other maintenance (including cleaning which involves the use of water or an abrasive at high pressure or the use of substances classified as corrosive or toxic for the purposes of regulation 7 of the Chemicals (Hazard Information and Packaging) Regulations 1993), de-commissioning, demolition or dismantling of a structure,

(b) the preparation for an intended structure, including site clearance, exploration, investigation (but not site survey) and excavation, and laying or installing the foundations of the structure,

(c) the assembly of prefabricated elements to form a structure or the disassembly of prefabricated elements which, immediately before such disassembly, formed a structure,

(d) the removal of a structure or part of a structure or of any product or waste resulting from demolition or dismantling of a structure or from disassembly of prefabricated elements which, immediately before such disassembly, formed a structure, and

(e) the installation, commissioning, maintenance, repair or removal of mechanical, electrical, gas, compressed air, hydraulic, telecommunications, computer or similar services which are normally fixed within or to a structure,

but does not include the exploration for or extraction of mineral resources or activities preparatory thereto carried out at a place where such exploration or extraction is carried out;

"contractor" means any person who carries on a trade, business or other undertaking (whether for profit or not) in connection with which he -

(a) undertakes to or does carry out or manage construction work, or

(b) arranges for any person at work under his control (including, where he is an employer, any employee of his) to carry out or manage construction work;

"design" in relation to any structure includes drawing, design details, specification and bill of quantities (including specification of articles or substances) in relation to the structure;

"designer" means any person who carries on a trade, business or other undertaking in connection with which he prepares a design, ~~or arranges for any person under his control (including, where he is an employer, any employee of his) to prepare a design, relating to a structure or part of a structure~~;

"developer" shall be construed in accordance with regulation 5(1);

"domestic client" means a client for whom a project is carried out not being a project carried out in connection with the carrying on by the client of a trade, business or other undertaking (whether for profit or not);

"health and safety file" means a file, or other record in permanent form, containing the information required by virtue of regulation 14(d);

"health and safety plan" means the plan prepared by virtue of regulation 15;

"planning supervisor" means any person for the time being appointed under regulation 6(1)(a);

"principal contractor" means any person for the time being appointed under regulation 6(1)(b);

"project" means a project which includes or is intended to include construction work;

"structure" means -

(a) any building, steel or reinforced concrete structure (not being a building), railway line or siding, tramway line, dock, harbour, inland navigation, tunnel, shaft, bridge, viaduct, waterworks, reservoir, pipe or pipe-line (whatever, in either case, it contains or is intended to contain), cable, aqueduct, sewer, sewage works, gasholder, road, airfield, sea defence works, river works, drainage works, earthworks, lagoon, dam, wall, caisson, mast, tower, pylon, underground tank, earth retaining structure, or structure designed to preserve or alter any natural feature, and any other structure similar to the foregoing, or

(b) any formwork, falsework, scaffold or other structure designed or used to provide support or means of access during construction work, or

(c) any fixed plant in respect of work which is installation, commissioning, de-commissioning or dismantling and where any such work involves a risk of a person falling more than 2 metres.

(2)   In determining whether any person arranges for a person (in this paragraph called "the relevant person") to prepare a design or to carry out or manage construction work regard shall be had to the following, namely -

(a) a person does arrange for the relevant person to do a thing where -
    (i)   he specifies in or in connection with any arrangement with a third person that the relevant person shall do that thing (whether by nominating the relevant person as a subcontractor to the third person or otherwise), or
    (ii)   being an employer, it is done by any of his employees in-house;

(b) a person does not arrange for the relevant person to do a thing where -
    (i)   being a self-employed person, he does it himself or, being in partnership it is done by any of his partners; or
    (ii)   being an employer, it is done by any of his employees otherwise than in-house, or
    (iii)   being a firm carrying on its business anywhere in Great Britain whose principal place of business is in Scotland, it is done by any partner in the firm; or
    (iv)   having arranged for a third person to do the thing, he does not object to the third person arranging for it to be done by the relevant person,
and the expressions "arrange" and "arranges" shall be construed accordingly.

(3)   For the purposes of these Regulations -

(a) a project is carried out in-house where an employer arranges for the project to be carried out by an employee of his who acts, or by a group of employees who act, in either case, in relation to such a project as a separate part of the undertaking of the employer distinct from the part for which the project is carried out; and

(b) construction work is carried out or managed in-house where an employer arranges for the construction work to be carried out or managed by an employee of his who acts or by a group of employees who act, in either case, in relation to such construction work as a separate part of the undertaking of the employer distinct from the part for which the construction work is carried out or managed; and

(c) a design is prepared in-house where an employer arranges for the design to be prepared by an employee of his who acts, or by a group of employees who act, in either case, in relation to such design as a separate part of the undertaking of the employer distinct from the part for which the design is prepared.

(3A)   *Any reference in these Regulations to a person preparing a design shall include a reference to his employee or other person at work under his control preparing it for him; but nothing in this paragraph shall be taken to affect the application of paragraph (2).*

(4)   For the purposes of these Regulations, a project is notifiable if the construction phase -

(a) will be longer than 30 days; or

(b) will involve more than 500 person days of construction work, and the expression "notifiable" shall be construed accordingly.

(5)   Any reference in these Regulations to a person being reasonably satisfied -

(a) as to another person's competence is a reference to that person being satisfied after the taking of such steps as it is reasonable for that person to take (including making reasonable enquiries or seeking advice where necessary) to satisfy himself as to such competence; and

(b) as to whether another person has allocated or will allocate adequate resources is a reference to that person being satisfied after the taking of such steps as it is reasonable for that person to take (including making reasonable enquiries or seeking advice where necessary) -
    (i)   to ascertain what resources have been or are intended to be so allocated; and
    (ii)   to establish whether the resources so allocated or intended to be allocated are adequate.

(6)   Any reference in these Regulations to -

(a) a numbered regulation or Schedule is a reference to the regulation in or Schedule to these Regulations so numbered; and

(b) a numbered paragraph is a reference to the paragraph so numbered in the regulation in which the reference appears.

Regulation 3   **Application of regulations**

(1)   Subject to the following paragraphs of this regulation, these Regulations shall apply to and in relation to construction work.

(2)   Subject to paragraph (3), regulations 4 to 12 and 14 to 19 shall not apply to or in relation to construction work included in a project where the client has reasonable grounds for believing that -
   (a) the project is not notifiable; and

   (b) the largest number of persons at work at any one time carrying out construction work included in the project will be or, as the case may be, is less than 5.

(3)   These Regulations shall apply to and in relation to construction work which is the demolition or dismantling of a structure notwithstanding paragraph (2).

(4)   These Regulations shall not apply to or in relation to construction work in respect of which the local authority within the meaning of regulation 2(1) of the Health and Safety (Enforcing Authority) Regulations 1989 is the enforcing authority.

(5)   Regulation 14(b) shall not apply to projects in which no more than one designer is involved.

(6)   Regulation 16(1) (a) shall not apply to projects in which no more than one contractor is involved.

(7)   Where construction work is carried out or managed in-house or a design is prepared in-house, then, for the purposes of paragraphs (5) and (6), each part of the undertaking of the employer shall be treated as a person and shall be counted as a designer or, as the case may be, contractor, accordingly.

(8)   Except where regulation 5 applies, regulations 4, 6, 8 to 12 and 14 to 19 shall not apply to or in relation to construction work included or intended to be included in a project carried out for a domestic client.

Regulation 4   **Clients and agents of clients**

(1)   A client may appoint an agent or another client to act as the only client in respect of a project and where such an appointment is made the provisions of paragraphs (2) to (5) shall apply.

(2)   No client shall appoint any person as his agent under paragraph (1) unless the client is reasonably satisfied that the person he intends to appoint as his agent has the competence to perform the duties imposed on a client by these Regulations.

(3)   Where the person appointed under paragraph (1) makes a declaration in accordance with paragraph (4), then, from the date of receipt of the declaration by the Executive, such requirements and prohibitions as are imposed by these Regulations upon a client shall apply to the person so appointed (so long as he remains as such) as if he were the only client in respect of that project.

(4)   A declaration in accordance with this paragraph -

(a) is a declaration in writing, signed by or on behalf of the person referred to in paragraph (3), to the effect that the client or agent who makes it will act as client for the purposes of these Regulations; and

(b) shall include the name of the person by or on behalf of whom it is made, the address where documents may be served on that person and the address of the construction site; and

(c) shall be sent to the Executive.

(5)   Where the Executive receives a declaration in accordance with paragraph (4), it shall give notice to the person by or on behalf of whom the declaration is made and the notice shall include the date the declaration was received by the Executive.

(6)   Where the person referred to in paragraph (3) does not make a declaration in accordance with paragraph (4), any requirement or prohibition imposed by these Regulations on a client shall also be imposed on him but only to the extent it relates to any matter within his authority.

Regulation 5   **Requirements on developer**

(1)   This regulation applies where the project is carried out for a domestic client and the client enters into an arrangement with a person (in this regulation called "the developer") who carries on a trade, business or other undertaking (whether for profit or not) in connection with which -

(a) land or an interest in land is granted or transferred to the client; and

(b) the developer undertakes that construction work will be carried out on the land; and

(c) following the construction work, the land will include premises which, as intended by the client, will be occupied as a residence.

(2)   Where this regulation applies, with effect from the time the client enters into the arrangement referred to in paragraph (1), the requirements of regulations 6 and 8 to 12 shall apply to the developer as if he were the client.

Regulation 6   **Appointments of planning supervisor and principal contractor**

(1)   Subject to paragraph (6) (b), every client shall appoint -

(a) a planning supervisor; and

(b) a principal contractor,

in respect of each project.

(2)   The client shall not appoint as principal contractor any person who is not a contractor.

(3)   The planning supervisor shall be appointed as soon as is practicable after the client has such information about the project and the construction work involved in it as will enable him to comply with the requirements imposed on him by regulations 8(1) and 9(1).

(4)   The principal contractor shall be appointed as soon as is practicable after the client has such information about the project and the construction work involved in it as will enable the client to comply with the requirements imposed on him by regulations 8(3) and 9(3) when making an arrangement with a contractor to manage construction work where such arrangement consists of the appointment of the principal contractor.

(5)   The appointments mentioned in paragraph (1) shall be terminated, changed or renewed as necessary to ensure that those appointments remain filled at all times until the end of the construction phase.

(6)   Paragraph (1) does not prevent -

(a)   the appointment of the same person as planning supervisor and as principal contractor provided that person is competent to carry out the functions under these Regulations of both appointments; or

(b)   the appointment of the client as planning supervisor or as principal contractor or as both, provided the client is competent to perform the relevant functions under these Regulations.

Regulation 7   Notification of project

(1)   The planning supervisor shall ensure that notice of the project in respect of which he is appointed is given to the Executive in accordance with paragraphs (2) to (4) unless the planning supervisor has reasonable grounds for believing that the project is not notifiable.

(2)   Any notice required by paragraph (1) shall be given in writing or in such other manner as the Executive may from time to time approve in writing and shall contain the particulars specified in paragraph (3) or, where applicable, paragraph (4) and shall be given at the times specified in those paragraphs.

(3)   Notice containing such of the particulars specified in Schedule 1 as are known or can reasonably be ascertained shall be given as soon as is practicable after the appointment of the planning supervisor.

(4)   Where any particulars specified in Schedule 1 have not been notified under paragraph (3), notice of such particulars shall be given as soon as is practicable after the appointment of the principal contractor and, in any event, before the start of construction work.

(5) Where a project is carried out for a domestic client then, except where regulation 5 applies, every contractor shall ensure that notice of the project is given to the Executive in accordance with paragraph (6) unless the contractor has reasonable grounds for believing that the project is not notifiable.

(6) Any notice required by paragraph (5) shall -

(a) be in writing or such other manner as the Executive may from time to time approve in writing;

(b) contain such of the particulars specified in Schedule 1 as are relevant to the project; and

(c) be given before the contractor or any person at work under his control starts to carry out construction work.

Regulation 8 **Competence of planning supervisor, designers and contractors**

(1) No client shall appoint any person as planning supervisor in respect of a Project unless the client is reasonably satisfied that the person he intends to appoint has the competence to perform the functions of planning supervisor under these Regulations in respect of that project.

(2) No person shall arrange for a designer to prepare a design unless he is reasonably satisfied that the designer has the competence to prepare that design.

(3) No person shall arrange for a contractor to carry out or manage construction work unless he is reasonably satisfied that the contractor has the competence to carry out or, as the case may be, manage, that construction work.

(4) Any reference in this regulation to a person having competence shall extend only to his competence -

(a) to perform any requirement; and

(b) to conduct his undertaking without contravening any prohibition,

imposed on him by or under any of the relevant statutory provisions.

Regulation 9 **Provision for health and safety**

(1) No client shall appoint any person as planning supervisor in respect of a project unless the client is reasonably satisfied that the person he intends to appoint has allocated or, as appropriate, will allocate adequate resources to enable him to perform the functions of planning supervisor under these Regulations in respect of that project.

(2) No person shall arrange for a designer to prepare a design unless he is reasonably satisfied that

the designer has allocated or, as appropriate, will allocate adequate resources to enable the designer to comply with regulation 13.

(3)   No person shall arrange for a contractor to carry out or manage construction work unless he is reasonably satisfied that the contractor has allocated or, as appropriate, will allocate adequate resources to enable the contractor to comply with the requirements and prohibitions imposed on him by or under the relevant statutory provisions.

Regulation 10   **Start of construction phase**

Every client shall ensure, so far as is reasonably practicable, that the construction phase of any project does not start unless a health and safety plan complying with regulation 15(4) has been prepared in respect of that project.

Regulation 11   **Client to ensure information is available**

(1)   Every client shall ensure that the planning supervisor for any project carried out for the client is provided (as soon as is reasonably practicable but in any event before the commencement of the work to which the information relates) with all information mentioned in paragraph (2) about the state or condition of any premises at or on which construction work included or intended to be included in the project is or is intended to be carried out.

(2)   The information required to be provided by paragraph (1) is information which is relevant to the functions of the planning supervisor under these Regulations and which the client has or could ascertain by making enquiries which it is reasonable for a person in his position to make.

Regulation 12   **Client to ensure health and safety file is available for inspection**

(1)   Every client shall take such steps as it is reasonable for a person in his position to take to ensure that the information in any health and safety file which has been delivered to him is kept available for inspection by any person who may need information in the file for the purpose of complying with the requirements and prohibitions imposed on him by or under the relevant statutory provisions.

(2)   It shall be sufficient compliance with paragraph (1) by a client who disposes of his entire interest in ~~the property of~~ the structure if he delivers the health and safety file for the structure to the person who acquires his interest in ~~the property of~~ the structure and ensures such person is aware of the nature and purpose of the health and safety file.

Regulation 13   **Requirements on designer**

(1)   Except where a design is prepared in-house, no employer shall cause or permit any employee of his to prepare <u>for him</u>, and no self-employed person shall prepare, a design in respect of any project unless he has taken reasonable steps to ensure that the client for that project is aware of the duties to which the client is subject by virtue of these Regulations and of any practical guidance issued from

time to time by the Commission with respect to the requirements of these Regulations.

(2) Every designer shall -

(a) ensure that any design he prepares and which he is aware will be used for the purposes of construction work includes among the design considerations adequate regard to the need -

(i)   to avoid foreseeable risks to the health and safety of any person at work carrying out construction work or cleaning work in or on the structure at any time, or of any person who may be affected by the work of such a person at work,

(ii)   to combat at source risks to the health and safety of any person at work carrying out construction work or cleaning work in or on the structure at any time, or of any person who may be affected by the work of such a person at work, and

(iii)   to give priority to measures which will protect all persons at work who may carry out construction work or cleaning work at any time and all persons who may be affected by the work of such persons at work over measures which only protect each person carrying out such work;

(b) ensure that the design includes adequate information about any aspect of the project or structure or materials (including articles or substances) which might affect the health or safety of any person at work carrying out construction work or cleaning work in or on the structure at any time or of any person who may be affected by the work of such a person at work; and

(c) co-operate with the planning supervisor and with any other designer who is preparing any design in connection with the same project or structure so far as is necessary to enable each of them to comply with the requirements and prohibitions placed on him in relation to the project by or under the relevant statutory provisions.

(3) Sub-paragraphs (a) and (b) of paragraph (2) shall require the design to include only the matters referred to therein to the extent that it is reasonable to expect the designer to address them at the time the design is prepared and to the extent that it is otherwise reasonably practicable to do so.

Regulation 14   Requirements on planning supervisor

The planning supervisor appointed for any project shall -

(a) ensure, so far as is reasonably practicable, that the design of any structure comprised in the project -

(i)   includes among the design considerations adequate regard to the needs specified in heads (i) to (iii) of regulation 13(2)(a), and

(ii)   includes adequate information as specified in regulation 13(2)(b);

(b) take such steps as it is reasonable for a person in his position to take to ensure co-operation between designers so far as is necessary to enable each designer to comply with the requirements placed on him by regulation 13;

(c) be in a position to give adequate advice to -

    (i) any client and any contractor with a view to enabling each of them to comply with regulations 8(2) and 9(2), and to

    (ii) any client with a view to enabling him to comply with regulations 8(3), 9(3) and 10;

(d) ensure that a health and safety file is prepared in respect of each structure comprised in the project containing -

    (i) information included with the design by virtue of regulation 13(2)(b), and

    (ii) any other information relating to the project which it is reasonably foreseeable will be necessary to ensure the health and safety of any person at work who is carrying out or will carry out construction work or cleaning work in or on the structure or of any person who may be affected by the work of such a person at work;

(e) review, amend or add to the health and safety file prepared by virtue of sub-paragraph (d) of this regulation as necessary to ensure that it contains the information mentioned in that sub-paragraph when it is delivered to the client in accordance with sub-paragraph (f) of this regulation; and

(f) ensure that, on the completion of construction work on each structure comprised in the project, the health and safety file in respect of that structure is delivered to the client.

Regulation 15   Requirements relating to the health and safety plan

(1) The planning supervisor appointed for any project shall ensure that a health and safety plan in respect of the project has been prepared no later than the time specified in paragraph (2) and contains the information specified in paragraph (3).

(2) The time when the health and safety plan is required by paragraph (1) to be prepared is such time as will enable the health and safety plan to be provided to any contractor before arrangements are made for the contractor to carry out or manage construction work.

(3) The information required by paragraph (1) to be contained in the health and safety plan is -

(a) a general description of the construction work comprised in the project;

(b) details of the time within which it is intended that the project, and any intermediate stages, will be completed;

(c) details of risks to the health or safety of any person carrying out the construction work so far as such risks are known to the planning supervisor or are reasonably foreseeable;

(d) any other information which the planning supervisor knows or could ascertain by making reasonable enquiries and which it would be necessary for any contractor to have if he wished to show -

(i)   that he has the competence on which any person is required to be reasonably satisfied by regulation 8, or

(ii)   that he has allocated or, as appropriate, will allocate, adequate resources on which any person is required to be reasonably satisfied by regulation 9;

(e) such information as the planning supervisor knows or could ascertain by making reasonable enquiries and which it is reasonable for the planning supervisor to expect the principal contractor to need in order for him to comply with the requirement imposed on him by paragraph (4); and

(f) such information as the planning supervisor knows or could ascertain by making reasonable enquiries and which it would be reasonable for any contractor to know in order to understand how he can comply with any requirements placed upon him in respect of welfare by or under the relevant statutory provisions.

(4)   The principal contractor shall take such measures as it is reasonable for a person in his position to take to ensure that the health and safety plan contains until the end of the construction phase the following features:

(a) arrangements for the project (including, where necessary, for management of construction work and monitoring of compliance with the relevant statutory provisions) which will ensure, so far as is reasonably practicable, the health and safety of all persons at work carrying out the construction work and all persons who may be affected by the work of such persons at work, taking account of -

(i)   risks involved in the construction work,

(ii)   any activity specified in paragraph (5); and

(b) sufficient information about arrangements for the welfare of persons at work by virtue of the project to enable any contractor to understand how he can comply with any requirements placed upon him in respect of welfare by or under the relevant statutory provisions.

(5)   An activity is an activity referred to in paragraph (4)(a)(ii) if -

(a) it is an activity of persons at work; and

(b) it is carried out in or on the premises where construction work is or will be carried out; and

(c) either -

(i)   the activity may affect the health or safety of persons at work carrying out the construction work or persons who may be affected by the work of such persons at work, or

(ii)   the health or safety of the persons at work carrying out the activity may be affected by the work of persons at work carrying out the construction work.

Regulation 16   **Requirements on and powers of principal contractor**

(1)   The principal contractor appointed for any project shall -

(a) take reasonable steps to ensure co-operation between all contractors (whether they are sharing the construction site for the purposes of regulation <u>11 of the Management of Health and Safety at Work Regulations 1999</u> or otherwise) so far as is necessary to enable each of those contractors to comply with the requirements and prohibitions imposed on him by or under the relevant statutory provisions relating to the construction work;

(b) ensure so far as is reasonably practicable, that every contractor and every employee at work in connection with the project complies with any rules contained in the health and safety plan;

(c) take reasonable steps to ensure that only authorised persons are allowed into any premises or part of premises where construction work is being carried out;

(d) ensure that the particulars required to be in any notice given under regulation 7 are displayed in a readable condition in a position where they can be read by any person at work on construction work in connection with the project; and

(e) promptly provide the planning supervisor with any information which -
(i)   is in the possession of the principal contractor or which he could ascertain by making reasonable enquiries of a contractor, and
(ii)   it is reasonable to believe the planning supervisor would include in the health and safety file in order to comply with the requirements imposed on him in respect thereof in regulation 14, and
(iii) is not in the possession of the planning supervisor.

(2)   The principal contractor may -

(a) give reasonable directions to any contractor so far as is necessary to enable the principal contractor to comply with his duties under these Regulations;

(b) include in the health and safety plan rules for the management of the construction work which are reasonably required for the purposes of health and safety.

(3)   Any rules contained in the health and safety plan shall be in writing and shall be brought to the attention of persons who may be affected by them.

Regulation 17   **Information and training**

(1)   The principal contractor appointed for any project shall ensure, so far as is reasonably practicable, that every contractor is provided with comprehensible information on the risks to the health or safety

of that contractor or of any employees or other persons under the control of that contractor arising out of or in connection with the construction work.

(2) The principal contractor shall ensure, so far as is reasonably practicable, that every contractor who is an employer provides any of his employees at work carrying out the construction work with -

(a) any information which the employer is required to provide to those employees in respect of that work by virtue of regulation 10 of the Management of Health and Safety at Work Regulations 1999; and

(b) any health and safety training which the employer is required to provide to those employees in respect of that work by virtue of regulation 13(2)(b) of the Management of Health and Safety at Work Regulations 1999.

Regulation 18   Advice from, and views of, persons at work

The principal contractor shall -

(a) ensure that employees and self-employed persons at work on the construction work are able to discuss, and offer advice to him on, matters connected with the project which it can reasonably be foreseen will affect their health or safety; and

(b) ensure that there are arrangements for the co-ordination of the views of employees at work on construction work, or of their representatives, where necessary for reasons of health and safety having regard to the nature of the construction work and the size of the premises where the construction work is carried out.

Regulation 19   Requirements and prohibitions on contractors

(1) Every contractor shall, in relation to the project -

(a) co-operate with the principal contractor so far as is necessary to enable each of them to comply with his duties under the relevant statutory provisions;

(b) so far as is reasonably practicable, promptly provide the principal contractor with any information (including any relevant part of any risk assessment in his possession or control made by virtue of the Management of Health and Safety at Work Regulations 1999) which might affect the health or safety of any person at work carrying out the construction work or of any person who may be affected by the work of such a person at work or which might justify a review of the health and safety plan;

(c) comply with any directions of the principal contractor given to him under regulation 16(2)(a);

(d) comply with any rules applicable to him in the health and safety plan;

(e) promptly provide the principal contractor with the information in relation to any death, injury, condition or dangerous occurrence which the contractor is required to notify or report by virtue of the Reporting of Injuries, Diseases and Dangerous Occurrences Regulations 1985; and

(f) promptly provide the principal contractor with any information which-

(i) is in the possession of the contractor or which he could ascertain by making reasonable enquiries of persons under his control, and

(ii) it is reasonable to believe the principal contractor would provide to the planning supervisor in order to comply with the requirements imposed on the principal contractor in respect thereof by regulation 16(1)(e), and

(iii) which is not in the possession of the principal contractor.

(2) No employer shall cause or permit any employee of his to work on construction work unless the employer has been provided with the information mentioned in paragraph (4).

(3) No self-employed person shall work on construction work unless he has been provided with the information mentioned in paragraph (4).

(4) The information referred to in paragraphs (2) and (3) is -

(a) the name of the planning supervisor for the project;

(b) the name of the principal contractor for the project; and

(c) the contents of the health and safety plan or such part of it as is relevant to the construction work which any such employee or, as the case may be, which the self-employed person, is to carry out.

(5) It shall be a defence in any proceedings for contravention of paragraph (2) or (3) for the employer or self-employed person to show that he made all reasonable enquiries and reasonably believed -

(a) that he had been provided with the information mentioned in paragraph (4); or

(b) that, by virtue of any provision in regulation 3, this regulation did not apply to the construction work.

Regulation 20   **Extension outside Great Britain**

These Regulations shall apply to any activity to which sections 1 to 59 and 80 to 82 of the Health and Safety at Work etc Act 1974 apply by virtue of article 7 of the Health and Safety at Work etc Act 1974 (Application outside Great Britain) Order 1989[1] other than the activities specified in sub-paragraphs (b), (c) and (d) of that article as they apply to any such activity in Great Britain.

1   *This Order has been replaced by the Health and Safety at Work etc Act 1974 (Application outside Great Britain) Order 2001/2127. As a result, CDM only applies to activities listed in article 8(1)(a) of the 2001 Order which do not involve work on or in connection with offshore installations, pipelines, pipeline works or mines.*

Regulation 21   **Exclusion of civil liability**

Breach of a duty imposed by these Regulations, other than those imposed by regulation 10 and regulation 16(1)(c), shall not confer a right of action in any civil proceedings.

Regulation 22   **Enforcement**

Notwithstanding regulation 3 of the Health and Safety (Enforcing Authority) Regulations 1989, the enforcing authority for these Regulations shall be the Executive.

Regulation 23   **Transitional provisions**

Schedule 2 shall have effect with respect to projects which have started, but the construction phase of which has not ended, when these Regulations come into force.

Regulation 24   **Repeals, revocations and modifications**

(1) Subsections (6) and (7) of section 127 of the Factories Act 1961 are repealed.

(2) Regulations 5 and 6 of the Construction (General Provisions) Regulations 1961 are revoked.

(3) The Construction (Notice of Operations and Works) Order 1965 is revoked.

(4) For item (i) of paragraph 4(a) of Schedule 2 to the Health and Safety (Enforcing Authority) Regulations 1989, the following item shall be substituted -

  "(i) regulation 7(1) of the Construction (Design and Management) Regulations 1994 (SI 1994/3140) (which requires projects which include or are intended to include construction work to be notified to the Executive) applies to the project which includes the work; or".
  [Revoked by the Health and Safety (Enforcing Authority) Regulations 1998 - Schedule 3]

Schedule 1   Particulars to be notified to the Executive

Regulation 7   1.   *Date of forwarding.*

2.   *Exact address of the construction site.*

3.   *Name and address of the client or clients (see note).*

4.   Type of project.

5.   Name and address of the planning supervisor.

6.   A declaration signed by or on behalf of the planning supervisor that he has been appointed as such.

7.   Name and address of the principal contractor.

8.   A declaration signed by or on behalf of the principal contractor that he has been appointed as such.

9.   Date planned for start of the construction phase.

10. Planned duration of the construction phase.

11. Estimated maximum number of people at work on the construction site.

12. Planned number of contractors on the construction site.

13. Name and address of any contractor or contractors already chosen.

Note: Where a declaration has been made in accordance with regulation 4(4), item 3 above refers to the client or clients on the basis that that declaration has not yet taken effect.

Schedule 2   Transitional provisions

Regulation 23   *(These provisions are spent)*

Appendix 2

EXTRACTS FROM THE MANAGEMENT OF HEALTH AND SAFETY AT WORK REGULATIONS 1999

Summary

1 The Management of Health and Safety at Work Regulations (the Management Regulations) place broad general duties on employers and employees in all non-domestic work activities. They aim to improve health and safety management and make more explicit what is required of employers under HSWA. The Regulations aim to encourage a more systematic and better-organised approach to dealing with health and safety.

2 Because of their wide-ranging general nature, the duties of the Management Regulations overlap with those of CDM. Where duties overlap, compliance with CDM will normally be sufficient to comply with the corresponding duty in the Management Regulations. However, where the duties in the Management Regulations go beyond those in CDM, additional measures are needed to comply fully with the Management Regulations. For example, the Management Regulations include particular requirements relating to young people, and the duties regarding co-operation are wider.

3 The Management Regulations place duties on employers (and in some cases, the self-employed) including those who are clients, designers, planning supervisors, principal contractors or other contractors.

4 Under the Management Regulations:

   (a) employers and the self-employed must assess the risks to the health and safety of their employees and others who may be affected by their work activity (regulation 3). This should enable them to identify what action to take to comply with legal requirements, applying the principles of prevention and protection (regulation 4). All employers must carry out a risk assessment, and those who employ five or more employees should record the significant findings of that risk assessment (regulation 3);

   (b) employers must make sure that there are appropriate arrangements for managing health and safety. This covers planning, organisation, control, monitoring and review of the preventive and protective measures. Employers with five or more employees must record the arrangements (regulation 5);

   (c) employers must provide appropriate health surveillance for employees whenever the risk assessment shows it is needed (regulation 6);

   (d) employers must appoint competent people, preferably their own employees, to assist with measures needed to comply with health and safety law and must provide them with the necessary information. Where more than one competent person is appointed, the employer must ensure adequate co-operation between them (regulation 7);

(e) employers must set up procedures to deal with serious and imminent danger, and danger areas, liaising as necessary with medical and rescue services (regulations 8 & 9);

(f) employers must provide employees with relevant information on health and safety, in an understandable form (regulation 10);

(g) employers and self-employed people sharing a workplace must co-operate with each other and co-ordinate the preventive and protective measures needed (regulations 11 and 12). Planning supervisors and principal contractors are particularly concerned with these issues;

(h) employers must make sure employees are not allocated tasks beyond their competence and physical capabilities and that they are provided with adequate health and safety training (regulation 13); and

(i) employers must provide temporary workers with appropriate/relevant health and safety information to ensure that they have the occupational qualifications/skills to carry out the work safely (regulation 15).

5 Employees also have duties, under regulation 14, to:

(a) use equipment in accordance with training and instruction;

(b) report dangerous situations;

(c) report any shortcomings in health and safety arrangements; and

(d) take reasonable care for their own health and safety and that of others who may be affected by their actions or omissions at work.

6 The remainder of this Appendix comprises extracts from the Management Regulations and its ACoP[13] cited in CDM ACoP. ACoP material from the Management Regulations is not additionally given ACoP status under CDM by its inclusion here. Schedule 1 referred to below means Schedule 1 of the Management Regulations.

Regulation 4   **Principles of prevention to be applied**

Where an employer implements any preventive and protective measures he shall do so on the basis of the principles specified in Schedule 1 to these Regulations.

29 Employers and the self-employed need to introduce preventive and protective measures to control the risks identified by the risk assessment in

order to comply with the relevant legislation. A set of principles to be followed in identifying the appropriate measures are set out in Schedule 1 to the Regulations and are described below. Employers and the self-employed should use these to direct their approach to identifying and implementing the necessary measures.

30   In deciding upon which preventive and protective measures to take, employers and self-employed people should apply the following principles of prevention:

(a) if possible avoid a risk altogether, eg could the work be done in a different way, taking care not to introduce new hazards;

(b) evaluate risks that cannot be avoided by carrying out a risk assessment;

(c) combat risks at source, rather than take palliative measures. So, if the steps are slippery, treating or replacing them is better than displaying a warning sign;

(d) adapt work to the requirements of the individual (consulting those who will be affected when designing workplaces, selecting work and personal protective equipment and drawing up working and safety procedures and methods of production). Aim to alleviate monotonous work and paced working at a predetermined rate, and increase the control individuals have over work they are responsible for;

(e) take advantage of technological and technical progress, which often offers opportunities for improving working methods and making them safer;

(f) implement risk prevention measures to form part of a coherent policy and approach. This will progressively reduce those risks that cannot be prevented or avoided altogether, and will take account of the way work is organised, the working conditions, the environment and any relevant social factors. Health and safety policy statements required under section 2(3) of the HSW Act should be prepared and applied by reference to these principles;

(g) give priority to those measures which protect the whole workplace and everyone who works there, and so give the greatest benefit (ie give collective protective measures priority over individual measures);

(h) ensure that workers, whether employees or self-employed, understand what they must do;

(i) the existence of a positive health and safety culture should exist within an organisation. That means the avoidance, prevention and reduction of risks at work must be accepted as part of the organisation's approach and attitude to all its activities. It should be recognised at all levels of the organisation from junior to senior management.

31   These are general principles rather than individual prescriptive requirements. They should, however, be applied wherever it is reasonable to do so. Experience suggests that, in the majority of cases, adopting good practice will be enough to ensure risks are reduced sufficiently. Authoritative sources of good practice are prescriptive legislation, Approved Codes of Practice and guidance produced by Government and HSE inspectors. Other sources include standards produced by standard-making organisations and guidance agreed by a body representing an industrial or occupational sector, provided the guidance has gained general acceptance. Where established industry practices result in high levels of health and safety, risk assessment should not be used to justify reducing current control measures.

Regulation 10   **Information for employees (see CDM regulation 17(2)(a))**

(1)   Every employer shall provide his employees with comprehensible and relevant information on-

   (a) the risks to their health and safety identified by the assessment;

   (b) the preventive and protective measures;

   (c) the procedures referred to in regulation 8(1)(a) and the measures referred to in regulation 4(2)(a) of the Fire Precautions (Workplace) Regulations 1997;

   (d) the identity of those persons nominated by him in accordance with regulation 8(1)(b) and regulation 4(2)(b) of the Fire Precautions (Workplace) Regulations 1997; and

   (e) the risks notified to him in accordance with regulation 11(1)(c).

(2)   Every employer shall, before employing a child, provide a parent of the child with comprehensible and relevant information on -

   (a) the risks to his health and safety identified by the assessment;

   (b) the preventive and protective measures; and

   (c) the risks notified to him in accordance with regulation 11(1)(c).

(3)   The reference in paragraph (2) to a parent of the child includes -

   (a) in England and Wales, a person who has parental responsibility, within the meaning of section 3 of the Children Act 1989, for him; and

   (b) in Scotland, a person who has parental rights, within the meaning of section 8 of the Law Reform (Parent and Child) (Scotland)) Act 1986, for him.

Regulation 13   Capabilities and training (see CDM regulation 17(2)(b))

(2)   Every employer shall ensure that his employees are provided with adequate health and safety training-

(b) on their being exposed to new or increased risks because of -

(i)   their being transferred or given a change of responsibilities within the employer's undertaking,

(ii)   the introduction of new work equipment into or a change respecting work equipment already in use within the employer's undertaking,

(iii)   the introduction of new technology into the employer's undertaking, or

(iv)   the introduction of a new system of work into or a change respecting a system of work already in use within the employer's undertaking.

(3)   The training referred to in paragraph (2) shall-

(a) be repeated periodically where appropriate;

(b) be adapted to take account of any new or changed risks to the health and safety of the employees concerned; and

(c) take place during working hours.

Appendix 3

THE CONTENTS OF THE HEALTH AND SAFETY PLAN

Pre-tender plan Regulation 15(3)	Construction phase plan Regulation 15(4)

The health and safety plan should include or address all the following topics, *where they are relevant to the work proposed.* Information in the pre-tender plan provides background information for those bidding for work, and for the development of the construction phase plan, which sets out how health and safety is to be managed during the construction phase. The level of detail should be proportionate to the risks involved in the project. The section titled *The health and safety plan* provides further information about the plan.

1. Description of project	1. Description of project
a) project description and programme details; b) details of client, designers, planning supervisor and other consultants; c) extent and location of existing records and plans.	a) project description and programme details; b) details of client, planning supervisor, designers, principal contractor and other consultants; c) extent and location of existing records and plans.

2. Client's considerations and management requirements	2. Communication and management of the work
▼ structure and organisation; ▼ safety goals for the project and arrangements for monitoring and review; ▼ permits and authorisation requirements; ▼ emergency procedures; ▼ site rules and other restrictions on contractors, suppliers and others eg access arrangements to those parts of the site which continue to be used by the client; ▼ activities on or adjacent to the site during the works;	a) management structure and responsibilities; b) health and safety goals for the project and arrangements for monitoring and review of health and safety performance; c) arrangements for: ▼ regular liaison between parties on site; ▼ consultation with the workforce; ▼ the exchange of design information between the client, designers, planning supervisor and contractors on site;

Pre-tender plan Regulation 15(3)	Construction phase plan Regulation 15(4)
▼ arrangements for liaison between parties; ▼ security arrangements.	▼ handling design changes during the project; ▼ the selection and control of contractors; ▼ the exchange of health and safety information between contractors; ▼ security, site induction and on site training; ▼ welfare facilities and first aid; ▼ the reporting and investigation of accidents and incidents including near misses; ▼ the production and approval of risk assessments and method statements; d) site rules; e) fire and emergency procedures.
3. Environmental restrictions and existing on-site risks	**3. Arrangements for controlling significant site risks**
a) safety hazards, including: ▼ boundaries and access, including temporary access; ▼ adjacent land uses; ▼ existing storage of hazardous materials; ▼ location of existing services - water, electricity, gas, etc.; ▼ ground conditions; ▼ existing structures - stability, or fragile materials; b) health hazards, including: ▼ asbestos, including results of surveys; ▼ existing storage of hazardous materials; ▼ contaminated land, including results of surveys; ▼ existing structures hazardous materials;	a) safety risks: ▼ services, including temporary electrical installations; ▼ preventing falls; ▼ work with or near fragile materials; ▼ control of lifting operations; ▼ dealing with services (water, electricity and gas; ▼ the maintenance of plant and equipment; ▼ poor ground conditions; ▼ traffic routes and segregation of vehicles and pedestrians; ▼ storage of hazardous materials; ▼ dealing with existing unstable structures; ▼ accommodating adjacent land use; ▼ other significant safety risks.

Pre-tender plan
Regulation 15(3)

▼ health risks arising from client's activities.

4. Significant design and construction hazards

a) design assumptions and control measures;
b) arrangements for co-ordination of on-going design work and handling design changes;
c) information on significant risks identified during design (health and safety risks);
d) materials requiring particular precautions.

5. The health and safety file

format and content.

Construction phase plan
Regulation 15(4)

b) health risks:
▼ removal of asbestos;
▼ dealing with contaminated land;
▼ manual handling;
▼ use of hazardous substances;
▼ reducing noise and vibration; and
▼ other significant health risks.

4. The health and safety file

a) layout and format;
b) arrangements for the collection and gathering of information;
c) storage of information.

Appendix 4

THE CONTENTS OF THE HEALTH AND SAFETY FILE

The health and safety file should include information about all the following topics, *where this may be relevant to the health and safety of any future construction work.* The level of detail should be proportionate to the risks likely to be involved in such work.

(a) a brief description of the work carried out;

(b) residual hazards and how they have been dealt with (for example surveys or other information concerning asbestos, contaminated land, water bearing strata, buried services);

(c) key structural principles incorporated in the design of the structure (eg, bracing, sources of substantial stored energy - including pre- or post-tensioned members) and safe working loads for floors and roofs, particularly where these may preclude placing scaffolding or heavy machinery there;

(d) any hazards associated with the materials used (for example hazardous substances, lead paint, special coatings which should not be burnt off);

(e) information regarding the removal or dismantling of installed plant and equipment (for example lifting arrangements);

(f) health and safety information about equipment provided for cleaning or maintaining the structure;

(g) the nature, location and markings of significant services, including fire-fighting services;

(h) information and as-built drawings of the structure, its plant and equipment (eg, the means of safe access to and from service voids, fire doors and compartmentation).

Appendix 5

FORM 10(REV)

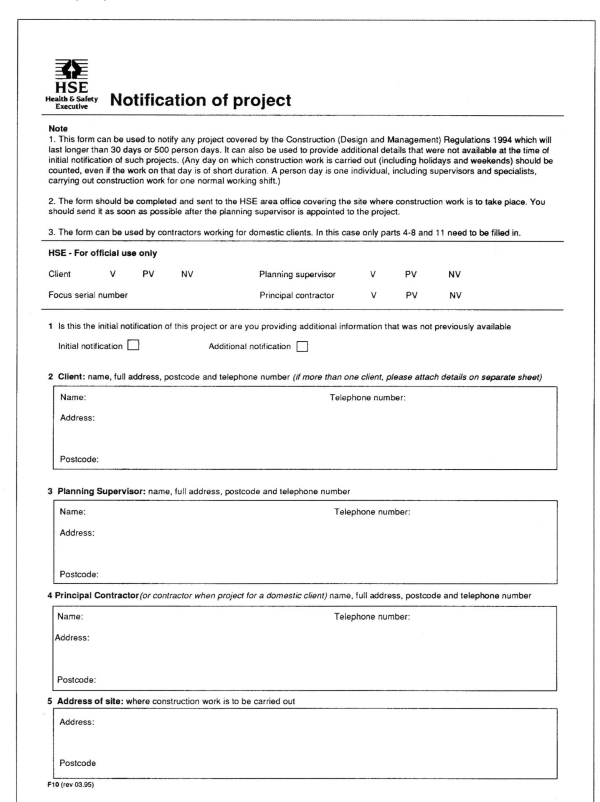

HSE
Health & Safety
Executive

Notification of project

Note

1. This form can be used to notify any project covered by the Construction (Design and Management) Regulations 1994 which will last longer than 30 days or 500 person days. It can also be used to provide additional details that were not available at the time of initial notification of such projects. (Any day on which construction work is carried out (including holidays and weekends) should be counted, even if the work on that day is of short duration. A person day is one individual, including supervisors and specialists, carrying out construction work for one normal working shift.)

2. The form should be completed and sent to the HSE area office covering the site where construction work is to take place. You should send it as soon as possible after the planning supervisor is appointed to the project.

3. The form can be used by contractors working for domestic clients. In this case only parts 4-8 and 11 need to be filled in.

HSE - For official use only

| Client | V | PV | NV | Planning supervisor | V | PV | NV |

| Focus serial number | | | | Principal contractor | V | PV | NV |

1 Is this the initial notification of this project or are you providing additional information that was not previously available

Initial notification ☐   Additional notification ☐

2 Client: name, full address, postcode and telephone number *(if more than one client, please attach details on separate sheet)*

Name: Telephone number:

Address:

Postcode:

3 Planning Supervisor: name, full address, postcode and telephone number

Name: Telephone number:

Address:

Postcode:

4 Principal Contractor *(or contractor when project for a domestic client)* name, full address, postcode and telephone number

Name: Telephone number:

Address:

Postcode:

5 Address of site: where construction work is to be carried out

Address:

Postcode

F10 (rev 03.95)

FORM 10(REV)

6 Local Authority: name of the local government district council or island council within whose district the operations are to be carried out

7 Please give your estimates on the following: Please indicate if these estimates are original ☐ revised ☐ *(tick relevant box)*

a. The planned date for the commencement of the construction work

b. How long the construction work is expected to take *(in weeks)*

c. The maximum number of people carrying out construction work on site at any one time

d. The number of contractors expected to work on site

8 Construction work: give brief details of the type of construction work that will be carried out

9 Contractors: name, full address and postcode of those who have been chosen to work on the project *(if required continue on a separate sheet) .(Note this information is only required when it is known at the time notification is first made to HSE. An update is not required)*

Declaration of planning supervisor

10 I hereby declare that .... *(name of organisation)* has been appointed as planning supervisor for the project

Signed by or on behalf of the organisation .... *(print name)* ....

Date ....

Declaration of principal contractor

11 I hereby declare that .... *(name of principal contractor)* has been appointed as principal contractor for the project. *(or contractor undertaking project for domestic client)*

Signed by or on behalf of the organisation .... *(print name)* ....

Date ....

Appendix 6

GLOSSARY

Term	Meaning
cleaning work	The cleaning of any window or any transparent or translucent wall, ceiling or roof in or on a structure where it involves a risk of a person falling more than 2 metres (see regulation 2 of CDM).
client	In this ACoP, client includes an agent, if one has been appointed.
construction phase health and safety plan	Arrangements for the management of the construction work to ensure the health and safety of all those involved or affected by the work.
contractor	An organisation or individual who carries on a trade, business or other undertaking in connection with which they undertake, carry out or manage construction work - includes sub-contractors. Regulation 2(1) of CDM contains the full definition.
demolition/ dismantling	The deliberate pulling down, destruction or taking apart of a structure, or a substantial part of a structure. It includes dismantling for re-erection or re-use. Demolition does not include operations such as making openings for doors, windows or services or removing non-structural elements such as cladding, roof tiles or scaffolding. These operations may, however, form part of demolition or dismantling work when carried out alongside other activities.
domestic client	A client for whom a project is carried out which is not related to the client's trade or business (whether for profit or not).
dutyholder	Someone who has duties under CDM.
fragile material	A surface or assembly liable to fail from the weight of anyone crossing, working, or falling on it (including the weight of anything that they may be carrying). Any surface or assembly may be fragile, particularly if incorrectly fixed, supported or specified. All tend to deteriorate with age, exposure to UV light and weathering. Typical fragile materials are roof lights, fibre cement sheets, corroded metal sheets, glass (including wired glass) and wood wool slabs. They present a risk to people installing the material, doing subsequent maintenance and crossing them to gain access to other parts of the structure, or plant situated on the roof. A test for fragility is set out in an Advisory Committee for Roofwork Material Standards publication: (ACR (M)001: 2000).[14]
hazard	Something with the potential to cause harm (this can include articles, substances, plant or machines, methods of work, the working environment and other aspects of work organisation). ACoP to regulation 3 of the Management Regulations[13] provides further details.

Term	Meaning
health and safety file	Information which people, including clients, designers, planning supervisors, contractors and others involved in carrying out construction or cleaning work on the structure in the future are likely to need, but could not be expected to know.
maintenance	The repair, renovation, upkeep, redecoration and high pressure cleaning with water or abrasives, or cleaning with corrosive or toxic substances of structures. The maintenance of services that are normally fixed to or within a structure is covered by CDM, but the maintenance of other fixed plant is not covered. The definitions of construction work and structure in regulation 2 provide more detail.
pre-tender health and safety plan	A plan containing the information required by regulation 15(3) of CDM, including information obtained from the client and designer, during the design and the early planning stages, for use by contractors, eg when preparing an offer to the client.
residual hazards/risks	The hazards/risks that remain after the design process.
risk	The likelihood of potential harm from a hazard being realised. The extent of the risk depends on: (i) the likelihood of that harm occurring; (ii) the potential severity of that harm, ie of any resultant injury or adverse health effect; and (iii) the population which might be affected by the hazard, ie the number of people who might be exposed. (ACoP to regulation 3 of the Management Regulations provides further details.)
Great Britain's territorial sea	This normally extends 12 nautical miles from the low water mark. Special provision is made where there are estuaries and bays.

A number of other terms are defined in regulation 2 of CDM (see Appendix 1).

Appendix 7

SUMMARY OF CDM DUTIES

CLIENT	CONCEPT AND FEASIBILITY	DESIGN AND PLANNING	TENDER/ SELECTION STAGE	CONSTRUCTION PHASE	COMMISSIONING AND HANDOVER
	So far as health and safety is concerned, ensure appropriate arrangements are made to manage the project (See paragraph 12 and HSWA)				
	Appoint a planning supervisor who is competent and adequately resourced for health and safety (See paragraphs 60, 73 and 193) (regulations 6(1)(a), 8(1)and 9(1))		Appoint a principal contractor who is competent and adequately resourced for health and safety (See paragraphs 60, 80 and 193) (regulations 6(1)(b), 8(3) and 9(3)	Ensure that when arranging for any contractor(s) to carry out or manage construction work, they are competent and adequately resourced for health and safety (See paragraphs 62 and 193) (regulations 8(3) and 9(3))	
	Provide the planning supervisor with relevant information to identify hazards (See paragraph 83) (regulation 11)			Comply with health and safety laws where client's work activities overlap with the construction work (See paragraphs 10 and 12-16) (HSWA, the Management Regulations etc)	
	Ensure when arranging for any designer(s) to prepare a design that they are competent and adequately resourced for health and safety (See paragraphs 77 and 195-6) (regulations 8(2) and 9(2))				
				Make sure the principal contractor's health and safety plan is suitable (See paragraph 88) (regulation 10)	Keep the health and safety file available for inspection (See paragraph 92) (regulation 12(1))

PLANNING SUPERVISOR	CONCEPT AND FEASIBILITY	DESIGN AND PLANNING	TENDER/ SELECTION STAGE	CONSTRUCTION PHASE	COMMISSIONING AND HANDOVER
	Ensure notification is submitted to HSE (See paragraphs 46 and 142) (regulations 7(1) and 7(3))		Ensure further notification details which were not known at the time of appointment are sent to HSE (See paragraph 49) (regulation 7(4))		
	If required, be in a position to give adequate advice to client on designer's competence and provision for health and safety (See paragraphs 142 and 153) (regulation 14(c)(i))				
	Ensure, so far as reasonably practicable, that designs comply with regulation 13 (See paragraph 142) (regulation 14(a))				
	Take reasonable steps to ensure co-operation between designers (See paragraph 142 (regulation 14(b))				
			Be able to give adequate advice to client on contractor's competence and provision for health and safety (See paragraph 153) (regulation 14(c)(ii))		
			Be able to give adequate advice to contractors on designer's competence and provision for health and safety (See paragraph 153) (regulation 14(c)(i))		
		Ensure pre-tender health and safety plan is prepared in good time (See paragraph 142) (regulation 15(1) to (3))		Be able to advise the client on the suitability of the initial construction phase health and safety plan (See paragraph 153) (regulation 14(c)(ii))	
		Ensure health and safety file is prepared (See paragraph 154) (regulation 14(d))			Ensure the health and safety file is delivered to the client (See paragraph 142) (regulation 14(f))

DESIGNER	CONCEPT AND FEASIBILITY	DESIGN AND PLANNING	TENDER/ SELECTION STAGE	CONSTRUCTION PHASE	COMMISSIONING AND HANDOVER
	Take reasonable steps to inform the client of their duties under the CDM Regulations (See paragraph 118) (regulation 13(1))				

Give adequate regard to the hierarchy of risk control when carrying out design work (See paragraphs 121-122) (regulation 13(2)(a))

Ensure design includes adequate information about health and safety (See paragraph 130) (regulation 13(2)(b))

Co-operate with the planning supervisor and other designers (See paragraph 134) (regulation 13(2)(c))

Ensure, when arranging for any designer(s) to prepare a design, that they are competent and adequately resourced for health and safety (See paragraph 116 and 193) (regulations 8(2) and 9(2))

Ensure when arranging for any contractor(s) to carry out or manage construction work, that they are competent and adequately resourced for health and safety (See paragraphs 116 and 193) (regulations 8(3) and 9(3))

PRINCIPAL CONTRACTOR				CONSTRUCTION PHASE	
				Ensure health and safety plan is prepared for construction work, monitored and kept up to date (See paragraphs 160-165) (regulation 15(4)), 16 and HSWA	
				Take reasonable steps to ensure co-operation between contractors (regulation 16(1)(a)) (See paragraph 167)	
				Ensure compliance with rules if these are made. (regulation 16(1)(b)) (See paragraph 171)	
				Take reasonable steps to ensure that only authorised people are allowed onto site (regulation 16(1)(c)) (See paragraphs 172-174)	

PRINCIPAL CONTRACTOR	CONCEPT AND FEASIBILITY	DESIGN AND PLANNING	TENDER/ SELECTION STAGE	CONSTRUCTION PHASE	COMMISSIONING AND HANDOVER
				Display a copy of the notification form (regulation 16(1)(d)) (See paragraph 175)	
				Provide planning supervisor with information relevant to the health and safety file (See paragraph 262) (regulation 16(1)(e)	
				May give directions to contractors and should monitor their work (See paragraphs 159 and 163-165) (regulation 16(2)(a))	
				May make rules in the health and safety plan. If they are made, they should be in writing. (See paragraph 171)	
				So far as is reasonably practicable, ensure information is provided to contractors (See paragraph 202) (regulation 17(1))	
				So far as is reasonably practicable, ensure contractors provide training and information to employees (See paragraphs 176 and 204) (regulation 17(2))	
				Ensure workers can discuss and offer advice and that there are arrangements for co-ordinating their views. (See paragraph 217) (regulation 18)	
				Ensure when arranging for any designer(s) to prepare a design that they are competent and adequately resourced for health and safety (See paragraph 158 and 193) regulations 8(2) and 9(2))	
				Ensure when arranging for any contractor(s) to carry out or manage construction work that they are competent and adequately resourced for health and safety. (See paragraph 158 and 193)(regulations 8(3) & 9(3))	

CONTRACTOR	CONCEPT AND FEASIBILITY	DESIGN AND PLANNING	TENDER/ SELECTION STAGE	CONSTRUCTION PHASE	COMMISSIONING AND HANDOVER
				Co-operate with principal contractor (See paragraph 182) (regulation 19(1))	
				Pass to principal contractor information which will affect health and safety, is relevant to the health and safety file or is relevant to RIDDOR (See paragraphs 182, 184 and 190) (regulations 19(1)(b), (e) and (f))	
				Comply with directions of principal contractor and rules in health and safety plan. (See paragraphs 182 and 185-187) (regulations 19(1)(c) and (d))	
				Provide information and training to employees (See paragraphs 183 and 206-213) (HSW Act, MHSW Regulations, etc)	
				Ensure when arranging for any designer(s) to prepare a design that they are competent and adequately resourced for health and safety (See paragraphs 182 and 193) (regulations 8(2) and 9(2))	
				Ensure when arranging for any contractors to carry out or manage construction work that they are competent and adequately resourced for health and safety (See See paragraphs 182 and 193) (regulations 8(3) and 9(3))	
				Ensure that projects for domestic clients are notified in good time (See paragraphs 50 and 188) (regulation 7(5))	

95

Further information

Key health and safety legislation is summarised below, along with abbreviations (where used). Note that this list is not intended to be exhaustive.

Health and Safety at Work etc Act 1974 (HSWA)
General duties to ensure health and safety of employees and others so far as is reasonably practicable

Construction (Design and Management) Regulations 1994, as amended (CDM)
Managing construction projects for health and safety

Construction (Health, Safety and Welfare) Regulations 1996 (CHSWR)
Specific requirements relating to construction work

Management of Health and Safety at Work Regulations 1999 (Management Regulations)
General management of health and safety including availability of health and safety advice and risk assessment

Provision and Use of Work Equipment Regulations 1998 (PUWER)
Machinery, vehicle and other work equipment suitability and safety, including safety helmets

Control of Substances Hazardous to Health Regulations 2002 (COSHH)
Control of health risks

Manual Handling Operations Regulations 1992
Control of risks from handling heavy and/or awkward loads.

Personal Protective Equipment at Work Regulations 1992
Provision and use of personal protective equipment

Noise at Work Regulations 1989
Control of exposure to noise

Confined Spaces Regulations 1997
Safe working in confined spaces, ie where there is a risk of death or serious injury from hazardous substances or dangerous conditions (eg lack of oxygen)

Lifting Operations and Lifting Equipment Regulations 1998
Requirements regarding the use of lifting equipment

Reporting of Injuries, Diseases and Dangerous Occurrences Regulations 1995 (RIDDOR)
Duties to report accidents, diseases and dangerous occurrences

Workplace (Health, Safety and Welfare) Regulations 1992 (Workplace Regulations)
General workplace issues, including some design requirements for commercial buildings

Health and Safety (Enforcing Authority) Regulations 1998 (HSEAR)
The demarcation between HSE and local authorities for enforcing health and safety law

Safety Representatives and Safety Committees Regulations 1977 (SRSCR)
The right of employees to participate, be consulted and represented on health and safety issues, including the appointment of safety representatives by recognised trade unions

Health and Safety (Consultation with Employees) Regulations 1996 (HSCER)
The provision of consultation for those employees who have no safety representative

Control of Asbestos at Work Regulations 2002
Control of exposure to asbestos

Control of Lead at Work Regulations 1998
Control of exposure to lead

Construction (Head Protection) Regulations 1989
Ensuring head protection is provided and worn

Electricity at Work Regulations 1989
Control of exposure to electricity

Statutory Instruments produced since 1987 can be viewed over the Internet at www.legislation.hmso.gov.uk/stat.htm.

References and further reading

References

1   *Successful health and safety management* HSG65 (Second edition) HSE Books 1997 ISBN 07176 1276 7

2   Evans, Haryott, Haste, Jones *The long term costs of owning and using buildings* R5.10 Royal Academy of Engineering Nov 98
    The Royal Academy of Engineering, 29 Great Peter Street, London SW1P 3LW
    Tel 020 7222 2688

3   *CDM Regulations - work sector guidance for designers*, CIRIA C604 Construction Industry Research and Information Association (CIRIA) 2004 ISBN 0 86017 604 5

4   *CDM Regulations - case study guidance for designers: an interim report* CIRIA Report 145 CIRIA 1995 ISBN 0 86017 421 2

5   *CDM training pack for designers* C501 CIRIA 1999 ISBN 0 86017 501 4

Available from: CIRIA, Classic House, 174-180 Old Street, London EC1V 9BP
Tel: 020 7549 3300, Fax: 020 7253 0523; website: www.ciria.org; e-mail: enquiries@ciria.org

6   *Designing for health and safety in construction. A guide for designers on the Construction (Design and Management) Regulations 1994* HSE Books 1995 ISBN 0 7176 0807 7

7   *Construction (Design and Management) Regulations 1994: the role of the designer* CIS41 HSE Books 1995

8   *Having construction work done? Duties of clients under the Construction (Design and Management) Regulations 1994* MISC193 HSE Books 1999

9   *Protecting the public: Your next move* HSG151 HSE Books 1997 ISBN 0 7176 1148 5

10 *Safety representatives and safety committees* [Codes of Practice and Guidance] L87 (Third edition) HSE Books 1996 ISBN 0 7176 1220 1

11 *A guide to the Health and Safety (Consultation with Employees) Regulations 1996. Guidance on Regulations* L95 HSE Books 1996 ISBN 0 7176 1234 1

12 *Home owner's information package* HB 14233/002. Available from the National House Building Council, Customer Services Department, Buildmark House, Chiltern Avenue, Amersham, Bucks HP6 5AP Tel 01494 735363 or 735369

13 *Management of health and safety at work. Management of Health and Safety at Work Regulations 1999. Approved code of practice and guidance* L21 (Second edition) HSE Books 2000 ISBN 0 7176 2488 9

14 *Test for fragility in roofing assemblies* (Second edition) (ACR (M)001: 2000). This can be ordered from: National Federation of Roofing Contractors, 24 Weymouth Street, London W1N 4LX. Tel 020 7436 0387

Further reading

CDM Regulations - practical guidance for clients and clients' agents C602 172 CIRIA 2004 ISBN 0 86017 602 9

CDM Regulations - practical guidance for planning supervisors C603 173 CIRIA 2004 ISBN 0 86017 603 7

Experiences of CDM Report 171 CIRIA 1997 ISBN 0 86017 479 4

A guide to managing health and safety in construction HSE Books 1995 ISBN 0 7176 0755 0

Health and safety in construction HSG150 (Second edition) HSE Books 2001 ISBN 0 7176 2106 5

Construction (Design and Management) Regulations 1994: the role of the client CIS39 HSE Books 1995

Construction (Design and Management) Regulations 1994: the health and safety plan during the construction phase CIS43 HSE Books 1995

Construction (Design and Management) Regulations 1994: the health and safety file CIS44 HSE Books 1995

A guide to the Construction (Health, Safety and Welfare) Regulations 1996 Leaflet INDG220 HSE Books 1996 (single copy free or priced packs of 10 ISBN 0 7176 1161 2)

Managing contractors: A guide for employers. An open learning booklet HSE Books 1997 ISBN 0 7176 1196 5

A guide to the Reporting of Injuries, Diseases and Dangerous Occurrences Regulations 1995 L73 (Second edition) HSE Books 1999 ISBN 0 7176 2431 5

RIDDOR explained. The Reporting of Injuries, Diseases and Dangerous Occurrences Regulations Leaflet HSE31(rev1) HSE Books 1999 (single copy free or priced packs of 10 ISBN 0 7176 2441 2)

Surveying, sampling and assessment of asbestos-containing materials MDHS100 HSE Books 2001
ISBN 0 7176 2076 X

HSE priced and free publications are available by mail order from HSE Books, PO Box 1999,
Sudbury, Suffolk CO10 2WA Tel: 01787 881165 Fax: 01787 313995 Website:
www.hsebooks.co.uk (HSE priced publications are also available from bookshops.)
Construction information sheets and free leaflets are also available on HSE's website,
www.hse.gov.uk

British Standards are available from BSI Customer Services, 389 Chiswick High Road, London
W4 4AL Tel: 020 8996 9001 Fax: 020 8996 7001 Website: www.bsi-global.com

The Stationery Office (formerly HMSO) publications are available from The Publications
Centre, PO Box 276, London SW8 5DT Tel: 0870 600 5522 Fax: 0870 600 5533 Website:
www.tso.co.uk (They are also available from bookshops.)

While every effort has been made to ensure the accuracy of the references listed in this
publication, their future availability cannot be guaranteed.

Printed and published by the Health and Safety Executive   6/04   C200